SURVIVAL

FROM CHILDHOOD SEXUAL ABUSE VICTIM TO WORLD BOXING CHAMPION

VINNIE CURTO
WITH DENNIS N. GRIFFIN

WildBluePress.com

SURVIVAL published by:
WILDBLUE PRESS
P.O. Box 102440
Denver, Colorado 80250

Publisher Disclaimer: Any opinions, statements of fact or fiction, descriptions, dialogue, and citations found in this book were provided by the author, and are solely those of the author. The publisher makes no claim as to their veracity or accuracy, and assumes no liability for the content.

Copyright 2019 by Vinnie Curto

All rights reserved. No part of this book may be reproduced in any form or by any means without the prior written consent of the Publisher, excepting brief quotes used in reviews.

WILDBLUE PRESS is registered at the U.S. Patent and Trademark Offices.

ISBN 978-1-948239-80-6 Trade Paperback

ISBN 978-1-948239-81-3 eBook

Interior Formatting/Book Cover Design by Elijah Toten
www.totencreative.com

SURVIVAL

Table of Contents

DEDICATION	5
ACKNOWLEDGMENTS	6
INTRODUCTION: By Dennis N. Griffin	7
PROLOGUE: By Vinnie Curto	10
Chapter One: Setting the Course	12
Chapter Two: Loss of Innocence	15
Chapter Three: Finding & Losing My Best Friend	27
Chapter Four: The Petronelli Brothers and My Escape	33
Chapter Five: Anchors Aweigh	39
Chapter Six: Miami Beach	44
Chapter Seven: Who Am I?	48
Chapter Eight: Turning Pro	55
Chapter Nine: Decisions	62
Chapter Ten: Another Marriage and a New Promoter	69
Chapter Eleven: Crossing Sammy "The Bull"	78
Chapter Twelve: François	83
Chapter Thirteen: Je t'aime	99
Chapter Fourteen: Canadian Sunset	106
Chapter Fifteen: Thailand—A Trip to Die For	114
Chapter Sixteen: Sly Stallone and Mustang Ranch	124
Chapter Seventeen: Another Brush with Death	130
Chapter Eighteen: Comic Relief	138
Chapter Nineteen: The Fight Is On	149
Chapter Twenty: The Countdown Begins	155
Chapter Twenty-One: The Final Test	161
EPILOGUE	167
PHOTOS	172
INDEX	179

DEDICATION

This book is dedicated to all victims of child abuse, whether emotional, physical, or sexual. I hope my story will encourage those who are suffering abuse, or have suffered abuse, to fight back. Don't endure your pain in silence. Break your abuser's hold over you by making your story public and holding him or her accountable.

Vinnie Curto

ACKNOWLEDGMENTS

I want to thank Barbara Seretan Gold, my companion and friend, for we have gone through a lot together, and without whom this book project would not have been accomplished.

My friend Ori Spado, your word is the best in Hollywood. You have done everything you said you would do, and have been there for me all the way. 1 thank you for getting Denny Griffin to be my great coauthor.

Anthony Spado, you're the best. I love you and thank you for everything.

Denny Griffin, thank you. I know you have had to pull extra weight while we were busy working on movie/TV stuff. I couldn't have done it without all your extra coaching! You're the greatest!

May God bless Mauricio Sulaiman and his late father, José Sulaiman, for helping me get my winning title shot.

I want to thank Rooshikumar Pondya for teaching me that love can conquer anything; François for teaching me you can learn to live and love again when you think all is lost; and the Seretans for introducing me to Lester Levenson and showing me such a powerful way to do all this.

Lastly, I want to thank all the kids who I have trained and mentored, who have constantly reminded me as the years have gone by that our time together in our simple boxing gym(s) turned their whole lives around! It certainly did mine, too.

INTRODUCTION

By Dennis N. Griffin

In the early part of 2015, I was contacted by an acquaintance dating back to my school days while growing up in Rome, New York. Orlando "Ori" Spado and I hadn't seen each other in decades, but he had heard from one of our former classmates that I had gotten into the writing business, with a focus on organized crime.

Ori explained that following an enlistment in the Army, he had become involved in organized crime as an associate of New York's Colombo crime family. He settled in the Los Angeles area upon being released from prison after serving a sentence for an organized crime- related conviction. He wanted to get his story out there and asked if I'd help him. I got on board and we began work on a manuscript we called *The Accidental Gangster*.

Shortly after that project got underway, Ori contacted me with another book idea. He had become friends with former super cruiserweight boxing world champion, Vinnie Curto. Would I also be interested in helping Vinnie with his biography?

My interest in boxing originated in the 1950s, when as a young boy I routinely watched the Gillette Friday Night Fights with my father on our black and white TV. Rome is near the village of Canastota, which is the hometown of Carmen Basilio, a former world champion in the middleweight and welterweight divisions. It is also the location of the International Boxing Hall of Fame. So, I definitely had an interest in boxing, but I had never before written about a sports figure. I reminded Ori that the current focus of my writing was organized crime and said I wasn't sure I would be a good fit for Vinnie. That's when Ori told me more of the details about Vinnie's life and the intended content of the book. I liked what I heard.

Vinnie's story had it all for me. Boxing, including the sleazy side of the sport, sex, drugs, and organized crime, both in the United States and Canada. Yes, I was interested. I told Ori I needed a little time to do some research on Vinnie and then I'd get back to him.

On June 11, 2015, Vinnie and I entered into an agreement that I would work with him on his book. Vinnie would provide the stories; I would research, edit, and organize. Because Vinnie had already written a substantial amount of material for potential scripts and various treatments, we got off to a fast start. After that, however, we experienced lengthy periods of inactivity. The main reason for the delays was the number of other irons Vinnie had in the fire. He was working on potential movie deals, training wannabe fighters and working with at-risk kids. These other endeavors took priority over the book.

During those down times I also turned my attention elsewhere—finishing old projects and taking on new ones. So, progress on Vinnie's book became a matter of when our schedules meshed. That day finally came, and we finished the manuscript. The total elapsed time for this project was just under four years, making it my longest lasting effort. And, I might add, one of the most gratifying.

Vinnie's life story is entertaining, powerful, and compelling. The chapters about Francois, the young Canadian boy who befriended Vinnie while he was hiding out from the Mob were especially emotional for me. When you read them, you might not come away with dry eyes.

I hope you enjoy reading this book as much as I did helping to write it.

PROLOGUE

By Vinnie Curto

My name is Vincent Joseph Curto. I was born in East Boston, Massachusetts, on July 10, 1955. I have three siblings, an older sister Maureen and two younger brothers, Wayne and Joey. My father, Jimmy Curto, was a raving, sick, alcoholic homosexual, and the jury is still out on my mother, Loretta Curto. They got married only to appease normal societal practices of the time.

I left home when I was fourteen to pursue a boxing career that I was brainwashed into by my father, but also to escape the hell of being sexually abused by him and his homosexual friends, along with the emotional abuse from my deviant, unloving mother.

Through boxing, I made what was considered large sums of money for the time at an early age, money that my father supposedly invested for me, which I never saw. I spent most of my adult life broker than the Ten Commandments. I made everything happen that was bad, and I ruined everything that was good. I actually died once and came back. I'm using that second chance to tell my story.

In these pages I'll lay it all out for you. You'll hear about abuse, the fight game, and the people I've dealt with both in and out of the ring. It's likely you'll find what you read to be disgusting, shocking, entertaining, or even humorous at times. When you're finished, you may like or dislike me.

That's okay, though, because this book isn't meant to be a whitewash. I'm giving you the facts and you can reach your own conclusions.

Regardless of what you think about me, there is one point I want to ensure comes through loud and clear—one paramount message I want to send. If you get nothing else out of this book, understand that child abuse in any form cannot be tolerated or condoned. If you're an abuser, please seek help. If you witness or suspect abuse you *must* report it. If you're a victim, absolutely fight back—do not let your abuser win.

Reliving my life while writing this book hasn't been easy and many old wounds were reopened in the process. Yet, if even one victim who reads it makes a stand and puts an end to the cycle of abuse, it will have all been worth it.

Please be advised that some of the names appearing in this book have been changed to protect individual privacy.

Chapter One

Setting the Course

"Asshole. Hey, Asshole," my father called to me. "You listen to me. You're a moron. You know it and I know it. But if you're Champ of the World, then you'll save me the embarrassment of calling you my son."

From as early as I can remember, my father called me Asshole so often I thought that was my name, until I started school and the teacher called me Vinnie. In spite of that and the other ways he abused me, I believe down deep he may really have loved me. At least that's what I like to think. He was so mentally and sexually deranged, consistently on booze, and hiding his homosexuality, that I think he truly didn't know how to show affection. Things were different back then. If my grandfather had known his son was a homosexual, he would have wasted him and started over. My father was able to keep his secret under wraps though.

My father was obsessed with me becoming a boxing champion. When I was seven, he came into my room with a gun. He held it out to me and said, "This is a thirty-eight revolver with hollow point bullets. Take it, Asshole. Come on, don't be afraid. Take it."

I took it from his hand and held it.

"Good," he said. "Listen close. If you don't win a title, you'll take that gun, put it to your head and pull the trigger. The bullet will enter your brain, ripping and mashing everything in its path. If you don't win a title, that's what you deserve. Don't ever forget it."

Then he took back the gun and laughed. I laughed, too, just to make him happy, but I wasn't laughing on the inside. That incident set the direction for my future. I was driven to do everything in my power to not have to put that gun to my head.

Shortly after that he started working with me, throwing punches at my head and body. I became very good at making him miss. By the time I was eleven, I was so good my father would take me out on the streets and have me fight with grown men—and I would often win. He even took me to barrooms and made me slap-fight with some of the drunks. I usually held my own, but sometimes they'd get carried away and end up hurting me. That didn't bother dad. He'd say, "He's gonna be the next champ; he can take it." My father would sneak up behind me and try and sucker punch me, and I somehow would find a way, with an awkward move or just barely make him miss, because I sort of developed a Jimmie Curto radar system. Many times, he'd fall flat on his face trying to hit me.

As a matter of survival, over time I became better and better at avoiding punches. Years later, my trainer, Angelo Dundee (who also trained Muhammad Ali and Sugar Ray Leonard), said I was a defensive genius. Thanks, Dad.

* * *

In the north end of Boston, right across the street from the Boston Garden, was a bar called Sharkey's. When we went there, dad gave the bartender his "He's gonna be the champ" spiel. The bartender said, "If you think he's that good, take him upstairs to the gym. They'll tell you if he's got anything."

We climbed four rickety flights of steps, with my father stopping on each landing to take a slug from his flask of

Seagram's Seven. When we got to the top, a sign on the door read, "New Garden Gym." There was a giant racket coming from behind the door. We went inside and these two big black guys were in the ring, boxing. I was afraid my father would want to match me with one of them and I'd probably get killed. Instead, he walked over to a rubdown table, took a couple of swigs from his bottle and passed out on the table. I was so happy, not realizing that in a professional gym, unlike my street and bar fights, they wouldn't have let me get seriously hurt.

While my father slept, I watched those guys box. They hit hard, fast, and with precision, things I wasn't used to. The trainer was standing outside the ropes screaming instructions to the fighters. When the bell rang, ending the round, they hugged and kissed each other on the cheek. The other gym members hollered compliments.

That scene caused a bright light to glow within me—I wanted to be a part of it. My feelings must have shown on my face, because a black guy standing on the other side of the boxing ring yelled, "Hey kid, you want to do this?"

I said, "I'd love to, but I don't have any money."

"Just show up. That's payment enough." He was Freddie Small, one of the trainers. I started going there every day, worked hard, and improved my skills. As the regulars got to know me and saw my work ethic, they gave me their accolades and eventually they became like family to me. It was my first experience with love, and I became addicted to it—I had to experience it every day.

In the gym I was in my element. The friendship and recognition I received caused me to drive myself even harder. I knew if I stayed with it I could become a champion. I'd make my father proud to call me his son, and I'd never have to pull that trigger.

Chapter Two

Loss of Innocence

There were always "hard guys" or gangsters around my neighborhood. I learned to tell one from the other. The hard guys were tough and played by their own rules when they wanted to get something done. The wise guys were an altogether different story. They were "with someone" who was powerful. If you fucked with them all hell would break loose and nobody, but nobody, could help you.

We lived at 191 Chelsea Street. My father was in the TV repair business and had his own shop called Jimmy's TV Repair. When alcohol and drugs eventually got the best of him, he lost the business. My mother didn't have a job outside the house and spent most of her time hanging out with her gay girlfriend, a super nice woman named Jeannie Casado.

A wise guy named Andrew Skip lived at number 189. He owned half of that block, but he didn't own the house that my family and I lived in. Our place was right next door to the corner coffee shop. Debbie's Coffee Shop was where the wise guys hung out, taking bets, taking numbers, loan sharking, and fencing stolen goods.

I figured out early that doing favors for them would benefit me. I remember one time the coffee shop got raided. I was only seven years old, but I knew there was a bag inside with all the betting and number slips, and the money—everything the cops were looking for. I walked into the store and asked for a sandwich. Rocky Memelo, the owner, said, "Oh, sure, as long as it's okay with the cops." The officers nodded.

I walked out with my sandwich, the bag containing all the slips and four grand in cash. The wise guys all loved me after that. When I started fighting in the amateurs, they were my biggest fans. Yet, as I grew up they let me learn the lessons of the streets, and made me stand up for myself.

* * *

I left the gym one day after a workout, feeling pretty good about myself and the respect I was earning from my peers. I was walking down Chelsea Street from Maverick Station when I stopped to watch these three kids showing each other how to box. These were big kids, one was about fifteen and the others were probably eleven or twelve. The fifteen-year-old was showing them how to box, how to use their hands.

As I walked by he said to his younger buddies, "Hey, go check out that little ugly guy."

I was little, and I might not have looked like it, but I could fight. The first young kid walked up to me to cause a problem. When he grabbed me, I hit him in the belly really hard and he fell to his knees. The other young one came at me next. He put his hands up and started jabbing, showing more skill than his friend. It didn't help him much, though. I out-boxed him, out-punched him, and chased him when he ran away. The third guy—the older one— tackled me and we started wrestling around on the sidewalk. I got him in a headlock and squeezed so hard he couldn't breathe. He begged me to stop. I let him go and he ran off. For the first time in my life I really felt that I was somebody, and my father wasn't there to laugh at the "Asshole."

Later that day, a local wannabe wise guy (not yet connected, but tolerated because he was trying to make his bones), in his mid-twenties named De Vito, came up to me and slapped me right across the face. He hit me so hard that my ears rang and my left ear oozed blood. It was the hardest I've ever been slapped in my life.

I questioned him, "What did you do that for?"

He said, "I watched what you did to those kids. One of them was my nephew, and I wanted to show you that you're not a tough guy at all."

Every day on the way home from school, De Vito would be on the street near the corner where I lived and I'd have to walk past him. He'd always give me a smack in my left ear or right ear. There were usually three or four local wise guys hanging around the corner. They'd see what he did, but never said anything. They would just shake their heads and go about their business.

That made me angry. They knew he was an adult and I was just a kid, and still they didn't help me.

After a few days I realized I had to deal with De Vito myself. I was smart enough to know a little kid doesn't have much of a chance against a grown man. So I went and got an alley apple, a cobblestone or brick found in the street rubble that weighed about twenty pounds, to even things up.

De Vito lived above the drugstore and had a side entrance to his place. When he left there to go to his corner hangout, he'd have to walk by the door to the drugstore. I stood at the entrance to the drug store with the alley apple over my head and waited. I could see the wise guys watching me from across the street.

I heard DeVito humming a song before he rounded the corner. I held the brick way up high, knowing if I missed I'd be in a world of shit. I did not miss, though. I caught him square in the face and the front part of his face caved in. He went down and out, but his legs were twitching like they had electricity shooting through them—I think I hit a nerve.

Even though he couldn't hear me, I remember screaming down at him, "How do you like it, you motherfucker? How do you like it? That wasn't my hand, you cocksucker, that was a brick."

I then kicked him three or four times.

A wise guy across the street hollered to me, "Scram! Somebody called the cops. The law is coming, and this guy could be dying."

I scrammed. De Vito hadn't seen who hit him and the cops never questioned me.

Six months later, I was walking across the street and there was De Vito. The scars on his face were still visible. He started toward me with that same mean look he had when he used to slap me. As he got near me he raised his hand.

The moment he did, I said, "What's the matter, you didn't get enough last time?"

I could tell from the look on his face the realization hit him like a *ton* of bricks, not just one! He put his hand down, walked by me, and said, "Get out of here." That was the last time I ever had a problem with him.

Some months later he was drafted into the Army and sent to Vietnam. Slaps and alley apples don't beat bullets. De Vito died in the battle at Hamburger Hill. I heard he had turned around and was real courageous.

* * *

The gangsters did help me some. Andrew Skip would pay me to clean up the alley behind the coffee shop. I liked the money, so if it wasn't dirty enough I'd make it dirty so he'd need me. He caught me at it one time. He had just checked the alley and I didn't know it. I messed it up and then told him it needed cleaning.

He looked at me and said, "Yeah? So go clean it—without pay!"

Before long I learned how to out-gangster the wise guys. I was watching them play poker one day and looked at everybody's hand. I whispered to Andrew, "You're gonna lose." He usually tipped me well for that kind of information.

On occasion, though, he didn't tip me. When that happened, the next time he gave me an "Am I going to win?" look, I'd shrug my shoulders like, "How would I know?" He'd start paying again.

This was the closest thing I had to fun in my childhood. The rest of it was pretty bad.

* * *

The sexual abuse started when I was eight. Maybe I should've seen it coming. The bizarre magazines my father had by his bed, showing men doing things to other men, should have tipped me off. Or perhaps seeing how close my father was with his friend Pudgy should have raised a red flag. What about the fact that I never saw my parents kiss or even touch each other?

Then again, maybe I did notice those things but ignored them because I wanted my life to be normal. It turned out to be anything but normal.

I remember my mother getting a call from the lady next door, warning that my father was staggering down the street toward home, drunk out of his mind, and ranting and raving to himself.

My mother ran to the front window and looked out to verify what she'd been told. Next she grabbed me, and then my brother and sister, and rushed us to the second floor and under the bed. It seemed we'd barely got there when we heard my father yell, "Loretta! Get down here and open this fucking door!"

That was followed by a loud crash as he broke through the door, and then creaking noises as he started up the stairs. They were the scariest sounds I've ever heard in my life.

My mother left us in the bedroom and rushed out to meet him at the top of the stairs. She said, "The kids are hungry. You drank up all the money—how am I going to feed them?"

"Fuck those animals," he screamed at her, and then cracked her across the face.

This was just one of many times that he hit her. To the day she died, my mother's nose looked just like mine, and I've had over a hundred professional fights.

Another time the neighbor called and said my father was on his way, but didn't look real bad. We were all relieved because it would be a peaceful night. He came through the door and up the stairs. There was no yelling or screaming.

He came into my room and said, "Vinnie?"

I was shocked that he called me by my real name. What was this all about? "Yes, Dad?"

"Did you go to school today?"

"Yes."

"Good. Good boy. Did you learn anything?"

"Not too much," I said, getting nervous from seeing a side of him I'd never seen before.

I wanted him to leave so I said, "I'm not feeling very well."

He said, "Daddy is going to make you feel real good. Don't you worry."

Now I was really confused.

And then he grabbed my pajama pants and underwear and pulled them down to my knees. He put his mouth on my private parts and began licking and sucking and I got an erection. I didn't fully understand what was happening, but I knew it was not something I particularly wanted from him.

When he was done, he asked me, "How did you like it?"

"Isn't this something you should do with Ma?"

He didn't answer me. He just walked out.

That was the first time he did a sexual act on me, but it was far from the last.

* * *

Alcohol and my father mixed in only two ways: with anger or sex. Time after time during his wild, drunken stupors he—and sometimes his friends—abused me. I'm not going to dwell on those many incidents because they were primarily similar in nature. However, I do want to tell you about a particular instance that is embedded in my memory.

I remember one night I was anxious for him to come home so I could show him an A-plus I'd gotten for a book report I'd done about Sugar Ray Robinson. When he finally showed up, he had Pudgy, and another guy I didn't know, with him. They were all drunk and belligerent, and my father was really nasty. Even so, I kept trying to show him the report. He wouldn't even look at it. He and his friends were only interested in one thing—having sex with me. If I resisted my father would hit me, he was a boxer in the Marines. The only good thing was, I would be so scared when they started doing things to me I would black out.

Even though I ran like hell to school the next day, I was late. When I entered the classroom all eyes turned to me. My teacher, Mr. O'Malley, paused as I took my seat in the back of the room by a large window with a view of the Boston Harbor.

I stared at the ships preparing to leave for the open seas. I dreamed of taking a trip with another family and going to a foreign land to live a different life—one with peace and love. Suddenly the bell rang, bringing me back to the present.

Mr. O'Malley said, "Mr. Curto, go on to your next class. I hope you learn something there, because you certainly didn't learn anything *here* today."

When I got up to leave I noticed my chair seat was covered with blood as a result of the actions of my father and his friends the previous night. Embarrassed, I sat back down.

Mr. O'Malley got agitated. He said, "Mr. Curto, what's wrong? I told you to run along to your next class."

I got up, wiped the seat clean with the bottom of my pants and ran out of the room.

The abuse began to happen more frequently. When I told my mother she covered for him.

"He didn't do nothing," she'd say. "You don't know what you're talking about."

My mistake was not telling others. My message to others is this: Whether the abuse has just started or has been ongoing, tell the truth and tell it to everybody!

I didn't, and I paid the price with my innocence and signed the tab with my blood.

* * *

I was thirteen or so, fighting three-round bouts as an amateur and doing well. However, what I was going through at home had me so disgusted and depressed that I began to eat all the time and started to put on weight. The only release I had was in the boxing ring. There, the anger I had toward my parents was unleashed on my opponents and I won five fights in a row. I was getting fat, though, and my inner rage was no longer sufficient to sustain me. I lost my next bout.

The legendary featherweight Willie Pep was there that night and talked with me after the fight.

He said, "Hey Kid, answer me one question. Do you know what you did wrong?"

"Yeah, I used it all up in the first round."

"That's right. You ran out of gas and had nothing left. You have to pace yourself. You didn't have a fight plan, either. You just went out there and went off like a bomb. That kid you fought is tough and he took your best shots. When that happens, what do you have to do?"

"Keep hitting him?"

"That's right! And I'm gonna get you back in the ring with him next week."

I was ecstatic.

Just as he promised, Willie arranged for the rematch the following week and he was right there in my corner. This time I fought smart, not angry. I paced myself, holding back a little in the first round, coming on stronger in the second, and letting it all out in the third and final round. Even the extra weight I was carrying didn't slow me down. I won all three.

My father was so excited about the win and that Willie had taken me under his wing, he spent the next few days calling everyone he knew bragging about me. While he was doing that, the molestation stopped. It stopped temporarily, but it didn't end.

It was time for me to get into organized boxing as an amateur.

* * *

I've probably had over two hundred amateur bouts in my life. I started training at the New Garden Gym at nine years old. They put me in the "novice division" at first; then at twelve, they put in the normal amateur division. I have to thank my father for one thing during that time. Probably the only reason I can still see straight today is because of the "collision avoidance system" he helped me develop by routinely hitting me with unexpected punches. Another unexpected gift I found at the Gym was the lifelong friendship and guidance of a part Indian, part Black young adult who trained at the gym, Ricky Wilkerson (now Ricky Simaratena). He took me to my ballgame, the Boston Red Socks at Fenway Park in Boston, one of the greatest experiences of my young life. Prior to this I usually only saw ball games standing outside of the TV shops (ours was usually broken). Fenway Park is outskirts of downtown

Boston. One of the walls is called "The Green Monster" and is the recipient of many of the world's greatest grand slams and home runs, the popular of which was "knocking one over" the Green Monster, out of the park! The view over one side was of all the big bank skyscrapers and the Prudential center. Carl Yastrzemski hit a home and then Rico Petrocelli got up to bat, and BOOM! Another home run. The crowd was going crazy. Next, Tony Conigliaro came up to bat….. you know what happened next….BOOM! Another home run. The crowd was going crazy and I was both in bliss from the game, and stuffed from all the hot dogs Ricky bought me. It was a preview of the great highs that sports would give me later in my life. I started fighting amateur, and Ricky would walk with me to my house afterwards. He couldn't believe how we lived and being the deeply compassionate man he was and is, determined to help me.

Freddie Roach, who later became the great Manny Pacquiao's trainer, was fighting in the amateurs with me. Freddie must have had parents who were a lot nicer than mine, because he had very little defense back then. He had a killer offense, though, a brilliant mind, and a big heart, both in and out of the ring. But his intelligence, mixed with the lack of a good defense, ended up with him eventually scoring one of the most coveted jobs in the world as Pac Man's main man.

Freddie Roach has remained a friend I have always been able to count on over the years to help me with a fighter or let me train at his Wildcard Gym in Hollywood. He never forgot where we both came from.

We used to go over to the Fargo Building in South Boston, the Irish part of town. The Navy had offices there, and I admired the naval officers in their uniforms who always looked so put together. They had a camaraderie I was always jealous of, too.

I made friends with everyone I could in my new life at the gym. Even with this big six-foot-four black fellow named

Val Boston, who absolutely hated white people. He hated them so much he wouldn't even wear anything white.

Freddie Small, who ran the gym, loved me but I wanted to feel that love with everyone I could. I felt bad for Val and wanted to win him over. I noticed he was crazy about normal gloves that you wear outside to keep your hands warm. He always seemed to have a different pair. One time he had a pair that didn't really fit. So, one weekend, I worked nonstop shining shoes at a quarter a pop and came up with enough money to buy him a really cool pair of black leather gloves with nice stitching. Freddie Small showed me where to get them.

When I gave the gloves to Val, he said, "What are these? Where did you get them?"

I said, "I bought them."

He looked one way and then the other in utter disbelief, and then asked, "How did you pay for them?"

I told him how hard I worked shining shoes because I really wanted him to have them. He looked up at the heavens and got all filled up with tears. He asked Freddie Small, "Did he really pay for these for me?"

Freddie said, "Yes, and he's a poor cat." Freddie had eaten at our house before, so he knew first hand my financial and family situation.

Val stayed silent every time I saw him for the next couple of days, but then he asked me to take a walk with him. He said, "When you get older, you'll understand a lot more where I'm coming from. I may have been mean to you many times (and he had been), but it's something I am facing in myself. It has nothing to do with you."

I was still in training when the Petronelli Brothers came to watch some of our amateur bouts. They saw me knock out my first opponent at twenty-eight seconds in the first round and were impressed. They came back to see my next three fights, all of which ended with knockouts (Kos) in the first round. They told me if I decided to pursue a boxing career to look them up when I was a little older.

A very valuable door had been opened.

Chapter Three

Socrates and Finding & Losing My Best Friend

Some days I didn't see my father at all because he was out getting drunk with his friends—those were the good times. Other days he'd come home early, drunk, and molest me—those were the worst days.

My mother's girlfriend was named Jeannie Casado. They'd go off together for hours at a time almost every day. With both of my parents gone most of the time, my older sister Maureen took care of us. I never had a father and son talk. I had no idea what it would be like to have a father who was also a friend.

When my parents were gone and it was just us kids in the house, I'd sometimes go into their bedroom and look around. On his nightstand there were books that I looked through and read some of them. Some of them were pornographic material on gay people; some were written by psychologists talking about sexuality and molestation.

However, the book I was drawn to was by Aristotle. When my father was sober, I'd often see him reading it. The pages were full of notations he apparently used to mark his favorite passages. One of the underlined areas was a speech by Socrates, who had been condemned to die by drinking a cup of poison hemlock. I read parts of the speech and a couple of paragraphs stuck in my mind.

"How you, O Athenians, have been affected by my accusers. I cannot tell but I know, so persuasively did they speak and yet they have hardly uttered a word of truth."

And, "Such is the nature of this accusation which has given rise to the slander of me, which in fact made them prepare these charges against me. I will sum up their words in an affidavit: 'Socrates is an evil-doer! And a curious person. He searches into things under the earth and into heaven. He makes the worst appear the better cause.'"

He also spoke about one God, equality, and peace when he made his final speech, and then drank the hemlock.

I read that when he was in jail, his followers broke in and tried to get him to leave.

They said, "Let's go, Socrates."

He replied, "I can't go. If I were to go with you, all my teachings would be for nothing."

He stayed.

I believe Socrates was searching for the truth and so was my father. I think what bothered my father the most was that he knew he was living a lie.

* * *

I told my father I needed a playmate and wanted a dog. I said I'd shine shoes to earn enough money to buy one. He said it was okay with him, so I started doing shines.

One night my father brought home a bunch of his drunken friends to play cards. When he came in he was carrying a shoebox that he stuffed into the kitchen garbage can and pushed it down. When he did, I heard a little squeal that nobody else seemed to notice. I figured one of the rats we had in the cellar must have come upstairs and got into the garbage can.

After the card game broke up, the men all left to go somewhere for a few more drinks. I waited a few minutes to make sure they were gone and then went to the garbage can. I'd been wrong. There wasn't a rat inside—there was a puppy in the shoebox! It turned out that someone had given him the puppy, but in his drunken stupor he had forgotten to give it to me and threw it in the garbage instead.

It was a female Labrador Retriever, small, cute, and cuddly. It was a case of love at first sight for me. Being that it was close to Christmas, I named her Jingles. My mother had Jeannie Casado and my father had Pudgy. Now I had a friend, too.

I shared my food with Jingles and fed her milk using an eyedropper. I raised her and took care of her. She was the best friend I'd ever had. She even seemed to know when I was feeling bad and would get close to me and lick me. I took her everywhere I went.

My father saw how much joy Jingles was bringing to me and how much I loved her. He didn't like it.

One day he said to me, "Asshole, where's that dog of yours? I've got somebody who wants her."

I said, "I can't give my dog away!"

"Yes, you can. You're going to be a man and give her away."

"But Dad, she's my best friend. She does everything with me. She won't know what to do with strangers."

"Enough! You're getting rid of her and that's the end of it."

The next day I took Jingles out for our regular walk. We went to the woods along the railroad tracks where there was a small unoccupied Civil War era jail I'd found months before. Inside, there was a bench, and there was a window through which I could see the Boston Harbor. I sat on the bench and hugged Jingles while I imagined being with her forever in a different family. I spent that night there with her and cried myself to sleep.

The next morning Jingles and I waited on the sidewalk in front of my house. When the guy who was taking her arrived, we walked over to him and I surrendered her.

When he tried to put her in the car she wouldn't go. Eventually he got her in and she scratched on the window trying to get out. It broke my heart and I burst into tears. As the car pulled away our eyes met. The message she sent me was, "Please, whatever I did wrong, I won't do again. Don't let him take me."

I cried harder. That was the last time I ever saw my best friend.

Days and then weeks went by. I was so lonely. I wasn't eating and was getting sick. I'd even been sent home from school for having dizzy spells.

When my father saw how bad I was doing, he said, "Hey, Asshole. What are you always blatting about? If it's over that fucking dog, forget about it. You're never going to see her again because dogs don't go to heaven. Here, read this book."

He handed me a book that said dogs can't get into heaven. Jingles and I loved each other unconditionally. Now I was told I would never be able to see or hug her again—not even when I died. My faith really suffered a hit that day, thinking God wouldn't allow dogs into heaven.

Some twenty-five years later, I was at a sports function to receive an award and a famous psychologist was one of the speakers.

I approached him and said, "Can I ask you a question?"

"Sure, go ahead."

"How come dogs don't go to heaven?"

He looked at me like I had two heads. "Who told you that?"

"My father."

"So, your father told you dogs don't go to heaven? When was your father anointed as keeper of the Holy Grail?"

"He wasn't, he just had a book that said that."

"Who wrote the book?"

"Some guy. I don't remember his name."

"Some guy, huh? I guess there *are* people who think they have a special hotline to God. Let me ask you this. Do *you* believe in God?"

"Yes."

"Is He the God of love?"

I nodded.

"Good. And you had a dog that was all about love?"

Again, I nodded.

"Please spell God backwards."

It hit me like a ton of bricks and gave me what I needed that day.

In 1989, a kid's movie came out, called *All Dogs Go to Heaven*. I ran to the store and bought the first copy of it on the stand, but to this day have never watched it, because nothing on a video tape could match my memories of Jingles.

* * *

As bad as my father was in so many respects, he did have an amazing talent I want to mention. It was a side of him few people knew.

The house we lived in had horrible electricity. Sparks would fly when you turned something on and there were lights that didn't work in the kitchen and parlor, where the TV was the only light in the room. To make matters worse, there was a big hole in the ceiling and in the winter my father had gotten several old electric heaters from somewhere to keep us warm, but only one of them worked.

One day he said to me, "Daddy's going to get the electricity straightened out in this house."

My mother overheard him and said, "What do you mean? You can't play around with electricity. You'll cause a fire!"

He ignored her and took me with him to the coffee shop next door to see Andrew Skip, the bookie. He asked to borrow fifty bucks. When Andrew wanted to know why he needed the loan, my father explained, "The electricity in the house isn't worth a shit. My kids are freezing and I can't get the electric heaters to work." Andrew gave him the money.

The first thing my father did was buy an electrician's code book. He took it in his bedroom and read it straight through. Then he bought some wire and tools and spent the next three days rewiring the house.

When Andrew Skip realized my father had rewired the whole house, he got nervous and contacted his own electrician to check out my father's work.

The electrician came over and said to my father, "Let me see what you did."

After looking everything over, the electrician said to him, "When did you get your electrician's license?"

"I don't have a license."

"You did this by yourself and you don't have a license?"

"That's right. I read an electrician's book and then I did the wiring."

"It looks like a professional job. You should have your own business."

The electrician reported back to Andrew and he came over with five or six of his friends. They found it incredible that my father could read a book overnight and be an expert on the subject matter the next morning.

What Andrew didn't know is that when my father put the fuse box in our cellar, he dug a crawl space over to the cellar of Andrew's coffee shop and hooked into his box. I don't know exactly how it worked, but we were able to get our electricity from the coffee shop.

Chapter Four

The Petronelli Brothers and My Escape

Pat and Goody Petronelli ran a boxing gym in Brockton, about twenty-five miles from Boston. Goody was the trainer, about forty-six years old, with a bizarre hairdo. Pat was about fifty and he was the boss. They had seen some of my amateur fights and, in 1969 when I was fourteen, they told me if I was ready to get serious about boxing, they'd get serious about me. I went to their gym where they evaluated my skills.

Goody said to Pat, "He's well-schooled."

"I can see that, Goody. He's got a very good left hand."

Then Pat said to me, "Vinnie, Goody and I like what we see. Right, Goody?"

"I can't agree with you more, Pat."

They seemed to enjoy saying each other's names and some people laughed about it. When it came to training fighters nobody laughed, though. They were the best in New England and I was happy they had accepted me and were considering me their top prospect. They kept a cot in the boiler room and even said I could sleep there if I wanted.

When I got home I told my parents I was moving to the gym, and left the next day with my few belongings.

One day Goody was holding my feet while I was doing sit ups and three black teenagers walked in. Goody said, "Did you guys come to box?"

One of them said, "Nah, we're here for the barbeque."

Pat appeared behind him. He either hadn't heard or decided to ignore the wisecrack. He pointed toward me and said, "Alright, you want to box? You can fight him. As a matter of fact, you all can fight him. Goody, get him ready."

Everybody put gloves on and I climbed into the ring. Jamal—the one who wanted a barbecue—got in with me. I made him suffer. Omar got in the ring next. He said to Jamal, "Man, you should be ashamed of yourself. That little white boy whipped your ass good."

The third guy hollered to Omar, "Don't be throwing all your shit right at the bell. Scope his ass out."

Omar nodded and then said to me, "I hope you know I'll be kicking your ass."

I beat Omar from pillar to post. As he stumbled from the ring he said to the last guy, "Don't do it, Stuff. Motherfucker isn't from this solar system." The kid got into the ring anyway, with a determined look on his face.

He came straight at me. I tattooed him with heavy shots and he answered with some shots of his own. I'm sure I would have gotten the decision if it was a real fight. But there was no quit in him. He kept coming and never made the same mistake twice. It seemed he got tougher with each minute that passed.

After the sparring session, Pat said to him, "What's your name?"

"Marvin, Sir, Marvin Hagler."

From that day on, Marvin was a regular at the gym.

* * *

Goody and Pat put Marvin and me to work in their construction company.

On our first day we were dressed in coveralls, standing on a scaffold painting gutters and totally ignoring each other. Al Green's *I'm so Tired of Being Alone* was playing on the radio. Instinctively, we both bopped to the music. There was an awkward moment as we each noticed the other grooving to the music. Marvin broke the ice by flashing a smile, causing our embarrassment to pass, and we began to sing along with Al. As much as I wanted to hate him, I couldn't. Marvin Hagler was cool people

One day Marvin said to me, "Vinnie, I'm going to show you how to get some furs."

It was payday and after work Marvin showed me what he was talking about. We walked the streets of Brockton and Marvin had me say seductive one-line comments to the girls when we passed by them.

He'd tell me, "Here come two furs. Hit 'em with your best shot."

I'd say to the girls, "Ladies, ladies, no need to fight. There is plenty of me to go around."

And that's just what they'd do—walk right around me.

After a while we decided to give the female population of Brockton a break and went to Dunkin' Donuts for a cup of coffee. We sat at the counter and Marvin said to me, "After I win the title I'll be swimmin' in fur."

I said, "When I get the belt, I'm going to pay my father back for everything he's done for me. I'm going to buy him a Mercedes Benz and a big house with my own bedroom."

Marvin said, "I've gotta get out of my place. I'm tired of watching my old lady drown herself in a bottle every night."

I said, "Yeah, that shit must suck."

Marvin nodded. "Fuck that bitch. When I win the title, I ain't givin' her shit."

I didn't say it, but I'd have taken his mother over my father any day.

Just then, a flamboyant transvestite named Tinkerbell floated into the coffee shop, wearing a green jumpsuit. Marvin's friend Omar strolled over to us and said, "Oh shit, get a load of Tinkerbell."

Tinkerbell glided past, giving me the once over and sat down a couple of stools away. Omar said, "Look out Vin, I think *it* likes you." Marvin and Omar laughed and high-fived.

Uncomfortable, I snapped, "Shut the fuck up!"

Tinkerbell removed a compact and powdered his nose, then turned toward me. "Excuse me," he said.

Reluctantly, I looked over.

"Do you have the time?" he asked.

I said "No" and turned my back to him.

Omar said, 'I told you he liked you. Maybe you two can double with me and my girl tonight."

"Shut the fuck up, or I'll throw you a beatin' like I did in the gym."

"Oh yeah? Don't sing it, bring it."

I jumped up, but Marvin restrained me.

Tinkerbell said, "Stop this instant!"

Then he pointed to me. "Young man, if you can't get along with them, you'll have to come right over here and sit by me."

Omar said, "Go head, your boyfriend's waiting."

I leaped off the stool, but I didn't go after Omar, Tinkerbell was my prey. I nailed him with a shot that sent his wig flying. He slumped to the floor, disoriented and in search for his wig. I was so angry I started kicking him and kept kicking him until he ran out the door.

I shouldn't have done it. But I was a fucked-up kid living in a frigging boiler room, and getting my balls busted about a guy like Tinkerbell made me crazy.

A few days later, Goody and Pat had me removing boulders from the cellar of a house we were working on. They were in a room on the first floor and I could hear them talking.

Pat said, "Goody, Vinnie isn't right in the head, you know."

"I disagree, Pat. He's okay and he has the potential to be a great fighter."

"You heard about him attacking that fag in the donut shop didn't you, Goody? Let's forget about him and concentrate on Kid Chocolate. Trust me, there's a future there."

I felt the blood drain from my face and felt so weak I had to sit down. I went back to the gym and stuffed my things into a pillowcase. I took a last look around the empty gym—a place where for almost two years I had felt loved—and then headed back to Boston and the waiting arms of my father.

* * *

A week later, I decided the only way I could escape was to join the Navy. I stopped in the recruiting office and was told because I was sixteen I was too young. The recruiter gave me some paperwork and said to have my mother or father sign it when I turned seventeen. I stashed the papers under the cushion on the couch and started counting the days. But the time came sooner than I thought.

One morning at around four o'clock, I was asleep on the couch in the living room when I heard the floorboards creaking. I stared into the darkness until my father emerged and sat on the couch.

He said, "Maybe there's a way out. I could go talk to the Petronellis and explain that you're sorry about that coffee shop thing."

As he talked his hand began caressing my thigh through the thin blanket. I said, "That's okay, you don't have to do anything for me."

I moved his hand but he put it back, this time under the blanket. He gave me the usual line, "Daddy just wants to make you feel good."

I sat up and said, "No! Not again. You're not doing that to me anymore."

I leaped up from the couch and ran into the kids' bedroom and slammed the door. He came after me.

I leaned against the door, holding it shut as he pounded on it trying to get in. My little brother Joey woke up and started crying. I heard my father hiss, "I said to open this fucking door!" It was a nightmare.

I began to pray to God for help. *Please God, make him stop. Please help me. He ain't gonna do this to me no more. No fuckin' more!*

Then I swung the door open, catching my father by surprise. I pushed him into the kitchen and then into a chair. I grabbed him by the throat with one hand and jabbed the index finger of my other hand into his face until I drew blood.

I shouted at him, "If you ever touch me again, I'll kill ya, ya fuckin' asshole!"

I stood there glaring at him until I felt the rage drain from me. As I continued to look at him I realized he was nothing—just a beaten man.

I knew it was time for me to get away for good. I left him sitting there while I went to the couch and got my Navy papers from under the cushions, brought them back and threw them on the table next to him.

I said, "Sign 'em, Pop, sign me up. If you don't, I'll tell your wife what you really spend your spare time on, besides drinking up all the money."

He scribbled his name and I picked up the papers and left. The next morning, the mother of a friend of mine who worked at the mayor's office and knew about my home life, fixed me up with some papers showing I was seventeen. My next step was the recruiting office where I submitted my paperwork and enlisted. I never looked back.

Chapter Five

Anchors Aweigh

I did my basic training in Great Lakes, Illinois, and that part of the Navy was a nightmare as far as I was concerned. Right after reporting in, all the recruits had to strip down, bend over, and be inspected for drugs. Believe it or not they found lots of drugs, but not from me. The good news was that my physical showed I was in top condition, unlike many of the others, most of whom had weight issues.

On a typical day we'd get up around dawn, have breakfast, do some marching, and then run an obstacle course. When you came to an obstacle, you were supposed to jump it. That was tough for some of the really overweight guys, so they'd run around them. They didn't get away with it, though. The instructors were always watching and made them go through the course again.

At the end of the course you had to go into a giant swimming pool by jumping in from a deck about sixty feet above the water and then doing a hundred-yard swim. Those reluctant to jump were pushed in by an instructor. If they couldn't swim, an instructor would extend a pole for them to grab and pull them to a ladder.

I was an accomplished swimmer and demonstrated all my strokes. With each one I told the instructor, "Sir, this is the left side stroke. Sir, this is the breast stroke. Sir, this is the butterfly. Sir, this is the freestyle."

When I finished, he was so impressed he assigned me to call cadence for the swimmers the next day.

The highlight of boot camp for me was when I met Dick Pettigrew, coach of the Navy boxing team. He wanted me on the team, but he ran into issues of his own and it was quite a while before I was able to join forces with him.

Some of the officers in boot camp were real Southern prejudiced guys. I had a fight with a couple of black guys who wanted their guy to get the bottom bunk, and I was determined to keep it. They made the mistake of getting physical with me about it, and one ended up on the floor, while the other went running down the hall. The officers were really interested, and when they figured it out about my age, tried to help me keep it covered up.

Admiral Zumwalt had heard about my boxing abilities and was trying to get me a fight for the Navy but was busy in Washington. In the meantime, I had to deal with his replacement, a junior officer who took a dislike to me. He told me, "You don't talk Navy or look Navy, Mr. Tough Guy. And I'll bet you're nowhere near as tough as you think."

One word led to another. Pretty soon he said he wanted to fight me to prove his point. It would be off the record and neither of us would get into trouble. I couldn't resist the offer and ground him into the pavement.

It turned out that in addition to being a lousy fighter, he was also a liar. He brought me up on charges. During the disciplinary proceeding it came out that my enlistment was fraudulent because I was underage at the time.

My brief Navy career was over.

* * *

I fought an amateur fight in South Carolina when I was discharged through one of boxing friends in Boston. It just so happened to be an Olympic year, so I tried out for the Olympic boxing team. As a bonus, Dick Pettigrew was one of the Olympic coaches. They said, "Oh, you're a Navy guy, Vin," and took me on their Olympic team. I started taking fights around the world during the elimination process.

When I was in South Africa there was a curfew for blacks. I came across a black guy who was out after curfew and was being beaten by some white guys. I went after the white guys and gave them a taste of their own medicine. I was proud of what I did. Despite everything, I still identified with myself as being Navy man, and we defended the defenseless.

Two of the other boxers I met on the National Tournaments were Duane Bobick and (Russell) Rusty Fickling, both great fighters. We hung out together. Bobick was six foot three and around two hundred seventy-five pounds. In spite of his size, it didn't take much alcohol to get him buzzed.

I was always a ball-buster, probably because of the suppressed hostility from my childhood. One time the three of us were in some hick bar in a local town. Duane drank six or seven beers and could barely talk, much less see straight.

A real nasty girl—four foot nine and around three hundred pounds, with rotten teeth, dirty hair, and a horrible odor—took a real liking to Duane. She wanted to know if he was interested in some sexual activity with her.

Duane whispered to me, "Is she nice?"

"Yeah, she's gorgeous," I lied.

They went upstairs to one of the rooms. After several minutes we heard Duane holler, "What the hell is that smell?" Then he ran down the stairs and out the door.

It seemed funny at first, but it turned out Duane caught something from her and for a while screamed in pain whenever he took a leak. He held that against me and we were never as close after that episode.

* * *

One of the matches we had while I was on the Olympic boxing team was in Miami, against the Cubans. I was matched against a prominent Cuban fighter and the famous trainer, Angelo Dundee, was in the audience.

When the bell rang to start the first round, the Cuban, who was a southpaw, came right at me and hit me with a straight left hand that sent me to the canvass. I picked myself up and somehow was able to finish the round. When I went back to my corner, the coach (not Dick Pettigrew) pleaded with me to take it to the Cuban and show him what the Navy was all about.

I listened, but when I went out for the second round, I fought my way—I decided to box, not brawl. I danced and moved, and every time the Cuban made a mistake, I nailed him with a flurry of punches. The crowd loved it. I won the last two rounds and got a split decision win. Unfortunately, though, we lost the overall match.

The coach came into the dressing room with me. He was all pissed off that I didn't follow his instructions and let me know it. In the middle of his tirade, Angelo came into the room.

The coach said, "Sorry, Angelo. We didn't perform the way we should have, but we're bringing in some new fighters and things will be different next time."

Angelo replied, "Well, whatever you change is your business, but I love the adjustments you made with Vinnie for those last two rounds. If plan A doesn't work, you've gotta go to plan B. The trouble with most fighters is they don't have plan B"

Then Angelo turned to me. "That was some good work, Vinnie."

I said, "I owe it all to the coach, here."

Angelo handed the coach a business card and said, "When Vinnie is done with the Olympics and wants to pursue a professional career, have him look me up."

After Angelo left, I snatched the card from the coach's hand. "I believe this belongs to me."

Later, Angelo sent me a letter telling me to come to Miami Beach and see him if I decided to turn pro.

Chapter Six

Miami Beach

Boxing was in my blood and I decided it was time for me to make my move. I headed for Miami Beach, looking for some boxing action, and went to the 5th Street Gym. I was toting my old duffle bag I got in the Navy, armed with the letter I'd received from Angelo Dundee.

There was a guy at the door—he couldn't have been over five feet, with a big nose, beady eyes, and smoking a cigar that seemed as long as he was tall. He said to me, "You gonna train today, Kid?"

I nodded.

"Okay. Emmett is my name, Sully Emmett. That'll be five beauties."

Waving Angelo's letter, I said, "I got this letter from Angelo Dundee. He told me to come down here and he'd help me turn pro."

A Cuban fighter who was shadow boxing nearby said to me, "Angelo's gonna take care of you? *Buena suerte, hermano* (good luck, brother).

Sully grabbed the letter from my hand and read it. "Why didn't you show me this when you first walked in?"

I shrugged and lamely said, "I don't know."

Sully walked me right back to the dressing room and into the toilet. He tacked the letter to the wall next to the toilet paper holder. He said, "You can stay here in the gym tonight and if you've got to go and the toilet paper runs out. Use that letter. That's what it's good for."

What the fuck?

"When will I be able to see Angelo?" I asked.

Sully laughed. "You'll see Angelo when he decides to stop in. That could be any time between now and never. Follow me."

He led me to the rows of seats surrounding the ring and I plopped down in the first row.

"Not there!" Sully yelled. "The front row is for big shots. You sit in the back."

As I got up to move, Sully stopped me and, with a twinkle in his eye, said, "Unless you've got a letter for that, too?"

I ignored his laughter and took a seat in the back. *Welcome to Miami fucking Beach!*

* * *

With no money and no definite appointment to see Angelo, I was either going to have to rough it on the streets until I bumped into him or go back home. I sure as hell wasn't going back to Boston, so the streets it was.

If you've got to live outdoors, you could do worse than Miami Beach. It was warm, but it was also very humid. In my duffle bag I had a couple of government issued blankets, my boxing gloves, and some clothes and underwear. When I left the gym that evening, I strolled down to the Fifth Street beach, which became my waterfront property.

Finding a spot in the sand, I rolled out my blankets and crawled into my bed, using my boxing gloves for pillows. The noise of the water gently lapping on the sand relaxed me and I was quickly asleep.

I woke up in the middle of the night soaking wet and freezing cold. The tide had come in and flooded my bedroom. That was the end of my sleep for the night—I was too cold and uncomfortable to doze off again. Besides, while

I'd been asleep, the beach had filled up with transients and I was sure there were some bad dudes among them. I closed my eyes and tried to at least get some rest, but after a few minutes I sensed someone near me. When I looked up there were three raggedly dressed homeless guys staring down at me like I was their next meal. When they saw me watching them they moved off. I didn't close my eyes again and dawn eventually came.

I was hungry and wondering where I could find a meal, when a car with a family in it towing a small camper pulled up and parked. I became engrossed in what unfolded next.

The father got out of the car, walked around to the passenger side, and took a young boy from his mother's arms. He carried him to the beach and sat the boy on the sand. He then sat down in front of his son and started to build a sandcastle, using his hands and a Styrofoam cup. He made three piles and then showed his son how to do the same. The little boy did one and then lost interest. His father tried to refocus him, but the boy wanted nothing to do with the project.

The father got irritated and refused to let his son off the hook. The kid rebelled and stood up on very unsteady legs. The father got excited, went to the car, and awakened his wife. She quickly joined her son on the beach, picked him up, and gave him hugs and kisses. Then the father went to the camper and returned with a little white puppy and the dog and the boy played in the sand.

I don't know the real story behind what I saw—I can only guess. I believe the child had some medical issues with his legs and when he stood up on his own it came as a surprise to his parents. In my mind they were a loving family that had just experienced what they thought was a miracle. I was deeply touched by it.

I got up, stuffed my damp blankets into my bag, smiled at the family, and walked off in search of a meal.

I turned down an alley next to a Food Fair supermarket. Across the alley from the Food Fair I saw the back of a restaurant. The door was open and I could see into the kitchen. I went by the restaurant's trash cans on the way to their dumpster, lifted the lid, and jumped in.

I'll tell you, Vinnie's restaurant had quite a menu: remains of baked potato with gum and scraps of sirloin steak with cigarette butts were only the beginning. I put the goodies into a bag and got back out onto the pavement. I didn't know it at the time, but some of the kitchen help were watching me through the open door. I took the food back to the beach, washed it, and chowed down, then went to the gym. This became my daily routine.

It turned out that some of the workers from the restaurant stopped by the gym sometimes to watch the fighters work out. One day, when I went to the dumpster, there was a bag on the top with "For Bennie" written on it (the Cubans weren't able to pronounce Vinnie). Inside there was a steak and mashed potatoes. Those beautiful people began leaving me stuff every day.

Sometimes when it got really cold at night I slept in the dumpster because it was much warmer than the sand. The rats didn't seem to mind and there was plenty of room and food for everybody.

Seven months later, after my first main event, I went to that restaurant through the front door and ordered a meal. This time the steak had no butts attached and the baked potato had no gum. When I got up to leave, the whole kitchen staff came out and gave me a standing ovation.

Chapter Seven

Who Am I?

My indoctrination into sexuality by my father had left me really confused. While in Miami and Miami Beach, before I turned pro with Angelo Dundee, I frequented gay night clubs like the ones my father took me to in Boston when I was a kid.

I was wandering the streets around six in the evening when I came across the Sausalito Club. I went inside, but the place was almost empty so I left and came back at a little before nine.

Things had changed in the interim, and when I was still a block away I could see a long line of people waiting outside the Sausalito's door. As I got closer I saw most of the people in line were ladies and a big guy was at the door deciding who got inside next.

I was wearing a tank top that showed off my muscular build. I started working the line, talking to the women who, from close up, appeared very macho. The doorman went up and down the line selecting people but kept passing me by. I told him it wasn't right because I'd been waiting longer than some of the people he was letting in. He walked right by me, so I went to the front of the line and went inside, where another doorman tried to stop me. I was ready to flatten him until he recognized me from the 5th Street Gym.

He didn't have my name quite right when he said, "Bennie Cooto, do you know what kind of a club this is?"

"Yeah, a nightclub."

He shrugged. "Sorry, Bennie, I can't let you in because the head doorman didn't pick you."

As we talked, I surveyed the crowd and realized it contained some of the ugliest women I'd ever seen in my life. One of them looked like Earnest Borgnine with a wig on. The head guy came in and grabbed me to throw me out. Before things went any further, this gorgeous young thing materialized and told the doorman I was okay and I was with her.

We went to a table and she introduced herself as Lulu. Before we could even order a drink, one of the bouncers came over and got right in my face. He told me I'd better behave myself because he was going to have an eye on me. If I did anything wrong he'd put my lights out.

I fired off a five-punch combination and he was out cold on the floor. The other bouncers raced over, removed their buddy, and surrounded me. Lulu again came to my rescue.

She said, "Okay, guys, you're better off not to approach this time bomb. Let me defuse it."

After that they left me alone.

I continued to frequent the club and develop my relationship with Lulu, often having sex with her. And then a cop who hung out at the gym wanted to talk with me.

He said, "Vinnie, Lulu was a guy and she had an operation."

"You're nuts," I told him.

And then he showed me an old mug shot of her as a man being arrested for prostitution. I was screwing a guy!

I told Lulu I knew the story.

She said, "Vinnie, I'm not gonna play with you. I think you always knew, but it made you more comfortable not to mention it because it brought back bad memories. Let me straighten you out, Baby. You're not gay, you're not a homosexual. You love it when I give you oral sex and you won't return the favor even though I had an operation. I know who I am and I gave up a job as vice president of a bank in order to be what I wanted to be. Go find yourself a woman that was born the way you like them."

I gave her a hug, walked out the door, and never looked back.

* * *

The next day I was in the 5th Street Gym when Angelo finally showed up. He remembered me and said, "Hey kid, I wanna see you work."

He had no idea what was going through my mind—no way of knowing what that meant to me or that since I'd come to town I'd been living on the streets, eating and sleeping in a garbage dumpster, and hustling transvestites. I knew all I needed was a chance to show what I had, and this was it.

I got my gear on and got into the ring to spar with this big black guy. The bell rang and he started pawing with a jab, bringing it back slow. I followed with a right hand-left hook combo that snapped his head back. That must have pissed him off because he started to unload on me. We stood toe to toe trading punches until I backed him into a corner. When the bell rang, we didn't stop, and the trainers had to come in and pull us apart.

Some guy asked me how I felt. I said, "I'm just getting started."

"Look at you, Jimmie Ellis is here, and you won't stop."

I said, "Jimmie Ellis is here?"

He said, "You just boxed Jimmy Ellis to a standstill." Ellis was a former World Boxing Association (WBA) champion.

Angelo liked what he saw and that was the day my career started.

I started training regularly at the gym. At first, I got a job as a dishwasher at Luigi's Italian restaurant across from the gym. The owner would come over to the gym and watch us work out. He let me sleep on a cot in the kitchen, a big improvement for me. No more sand in my teeth, my nose, my hair. At the same time, my friend Ricky from Boston was worried about me and came down to train some and keep an eye on me. Ricky always lifted my spirits, which were already in the best shape in years, and with both of us working at Luigi's kitchen, I always had tons of food to eat.

After a while, Angelo started paying for me to stay at the Miami Beach Hotel and said he would take it out of my pay when I fought a main event. I thought I died and went to heaven.

One day when we were training, Ali came to train for one of his fights. I was a regular by then and when Ali came, they threw everyone but us regulars out. My friend Mickey, who was a student at Miami University, wanted to stay and watch. I got Angelo to let him stay, and Angelo laughingly made him go into the ring and play around with Ali. The cameras were rolling, and Ali was talking shit to him, "Show me what you got, sucker!"

Mickey didn't realize how good he looked in there. He was in such awe of Ali that he was in kind of a daze that lasted for days. My friend's full name is Mickey Rourke, the superstar actor. Being in the ring with Ali is something he never forgot. To this day, he tells me if I ever want him to play a role in one of my projects, he'll be there.

* * *

Following his March 8, 1971, loss to Joe Frazier, Muhammad Ali began fighting his way back into title contention. In early 1972, Angelo said to me. "Ali is getting ready for another fight, so I won't be able to see much of you around here. How would you like to come to Ali's training camp with me?"

I was speechless. The thought of going to training camp with the greatest heavyweight champion to ever lace on a set of gloves was overwhelming. I could barely sleep the two nights before we left for the camp, which was located on a mountain in Deer Lake, Pennsylvania.

When we arrived, Ali's assistant trainer and corner man Drew Bundini Brown took me to a small cabin where I'd be staying. There were four or five similar cabins for sparring partners, friends and members of the press. There was a big mess hall in the middle of the compound where a sweet little lady Ali called "Aunt Coretta" did the cooking.

Excited, I called my father and said I was in a place that was truly a fighter's heaven. Ali was a prankster and joked around a lot. He didn't let anyone take themselves too seriously. He made sure the atmosphere was light and fun. Once he put on a bear costume and scared the heck out of a bunch of us—chasing us all over until we finally realized it was him.

We got up around four-thirty every morning and Ali would lead us on a run down the mountain and then we'd jog along the road. Each day about twenty-five minutes into the run, traffic would be backed up a long way with people wanting to get a glimpse of their beloved champ.

Another thing about Ali's camp was that he would bring extraordinary people in all the time because he wanted to meet the most gifted people from around the world. He had this guy from India, or maybe some other planet, visit us. The guy could heal people by touching them or could make metal dissolve.

Ali let the guy use his gold ring with a large stone as a test. The Indian grabbed Ali's hand, pulled it to his chest, and closed his eyes. Tears poured down his face and as he released Ali's hand several seconds later, the stone dropped to the ground and the metal dissolved into liquid.

Ali was amazed. He laughed and said, "If I was to fight you, you'd probably dissolve my arm."

The Indian said, "It shows you the power of Divine Love."

From what I know of Ali, he had plenty of love. He cared for people in general and made sure his sparring partners, such as Ken Norton, Ron Lyle, Earnie Shavers, and Larry Holmes, were treated right. He had Angelo get them the right fights to bring them up to a level of skill where they had the best chance to win.

Anyway, I was learning a lot and having the time of my life.

I was worried that had changed one day, though, when I told Ali about a book my father had in which it said that blacks used to be paid more money than Italian immigrants for digging ditches. Ali felt that was insulting and blew his stack. I thought he was going to hit me. He wanted to see the book for himself, so he called my father, got the name of the book, ordered a copy, and had it flown in a day or two later.

A few afternoons later, Ali loaded all the fighters into his RV and drove us to a college campus where he was scheduled to give a talk.

After speaking to the students, he introduced all us fighters to the audience. When he got to me, he said, "Every man is my teacher. This young fighter taught me something today about my own people. I was wrong and he was right. I predict he is going to be a world champion one day."

I will proudly take that moment to the grave with me. I'll never forget it and I'll never forget Muhammad Ali. He was a great fighter and a great man, as well.

* * *

It was at this time I met my first wife—the first of six. Her name was Marina, a beautiful Cuban girl I met at the Fifth Street Gym before I turned pro. She was doing a report on sports for a school project and it was lust at first sight.

We got married right away, before we were anywhere near ready.

One day I got into an argument with Chuck Talhami (who was helping with my training) about when I'd be ready to go against better fighters—I thought it was time, he didn't. Things got pretty heated.

Back at our apartment after the argument, Marina tried to comfort me by telling me I didn't have to fight for a living. If I wanted to quit, her father would give me a job in his factory. She meant well, but that only made me madder. The thought of giving up my goal of becoming a champion to work in a factory was insulting to me, and I told her so.

In the middle of our spat, her father showed up. I told him, "I don't want any part of your business. I'm gonna be a champ someday, and if you don't believe in me, you and Marina can both fuck off."

Marina broke into tears and her father pulled out a silver pistol and started shooting at me. I jumped out the second story window and hit the ground running. I heard a couple of bullets whiz by fairly close as I made my escape.

That was the end of the marriage. I got a divorce through the mail and never saw Marina again. With her out of the picture, I renewed my focus on boxing.

Chapter Eight

Turning Pro

On October 10, 1972, under Angelo's tutelage and after only a few amateur fights, I had my first pro bout against a guy named Victor Taco Perez. Angelo, Chuck Talhami, and Moe Fleischer were in my corner that night. I won by TKO (technical knockout) at the end of the fifth round.

Chuck had originally come to the gym to work with his brother Eddie, but they messed up big time with Eddie, pushed him too soon and got him in over his head. But Chuck and I worked well together and were about the only non-Cuban and non-Jewish guys around.

I loved Chuck, but I tortured him sometimes. He would try to force me to spend more time in the steam room to keep my weight down, and I would say, "No, I hate the steam room. I'm weak enough from starving myself."

He'd come back with, "You must do this for your career, for your life."

I still refused.

Another time when we were staying in a hotel, Chuck was just out of the shower and was still nude when I said to him, "I left my hat on the outside doorknob. Reach out and grab it, will you?"

When he opened the door to stick his hand out, I pushed him the rest of the way into the hallway and locked the door.

I heard a little knock, then, "Vinnie, I swear to God, if you love God, by my father's grave, open this door."

Then I heard a woman shrieking, "A naked man! There's a naked man!"

Chuck yelled through the door, "You bastard! Open this door or I won't train you anymore."

I let him back in, but I pulled many more similar stunts on him.

* * *

One day in the gym, a young Latino with green eyes and wearing a silk suit came up to me and playfully threw some combinations in the air. His name was Charlie Migola; we talked a while and became friends.

We went out one night to the Fontainebleau Hotel; and then Charlie took me out to an enormous yacht anchored in the harbor to meet his uncle. On the way we passed a group of provocatively dressed beauties and I wanted to stop and get acquainted. Charlie laughed and said, "Don't worry, they aren't going anywhere. They're all paid for."

Onboard, music was blaring. Some coked-out partiers danced while other more serious guests played backgammon for large stakes.

Passing through the crowd, we approached a group of sophisticated looking men reclining on lounge chairs and sipping champagne. In the center of the group was Roberto Migola, about forty years old, with dark curly hair and a ruddy complexion. He was a big shot in a South American drug cartel.

Charlie made the introduction and Roberto shook my hand. He said he'd seen me fight in Miami Beach and admired my abilities. His only criticism was that I didn't go to my opponent's body earlier. I told him I'd keep that in mind for the future because I never knew when I'd fight the same guy again.

Roberto said, "That's the same way I am in my business." Everyone chuckled.

Charlie noticed my eyes wandering to the topless hookers who were packing their noses with coke as they danced.

He said to his uncle, "I think Vinnie sees a few old friends he hasn't met yet."

Roberto nodded and laughed. He said, "Don't just look, Vinnie. Help yourself."

It was quite a night.

* * *

Angelo was a great motivator and he showed me that in my second fight, on January 30, 1973. Angelo's brother Chris set up the matches and the guy he had paired me with backed out. His replacement was a real banger named Dave Lee Royster. In the opening round, I hit him with everything I had, but he wouldn't go down. In fact, he came right back at me with some ferocious punches and caught me good a couple of times.

When I got back to the corner, I was pretty disgusted and wondering if fighting Royster was a mistake. As soon as I got on my stool, Angelo threw a giant bucket of ice on me. Then he slapped me in the face and said, "This guy wants to quit. Now you go back in there and *make* him quit." I knocked Royster out in the fourth round.

I soon started sparring with a guy named Vernon McIntosh. He could box a little, punch like Joe Lewis with either hand, and had a chin like steel. He and my friend Ricky, who had come down to Miami Beach to keep an eye on me, hung out and had the most fun I had had in years.

Vern was the kindest, sweetest kid, but not the sharpest tool in the shed. He was another fighter ruined by his manager putting him in with heavy hitters before he was ready. Unfortunately, there are a lot of fighters like Vern in the boxing business.

* * *

On June 19, 1973, in my tenth fight, I fought my first main event—a ten-rounder against a light heavyweight named Casey Gacic. I'd been having trouble making weight and watched anxiously as the boxing commissioner tapped the balance weight higher and higher. "One hundred eighty," he announced. I was two fucking pounds over. "You've got three hours to make weight," the commissioner added.

Angelo was really disappointed in me and Chuck asked me if I really wanted to be a champion. Depressed, I went to the nearest sweat room, put on layers of sweats, and slumped down on the bench. My friend Charlie stood over me in red bikini briefs, dancing around and shadow boxing. Suddenly he said, "Get up, I know what to do."

When I was on my feet he started singing something with a cha-cha beat. He said, "Echa pa'lante, echa pa'trás, oye la música, la cha cha cha!!! Come on, start dancing."

We danced around the room for over two hours and I thought I was on the verge of collapse. It paid off, though, and when I went back on the scale I was down to one-seventy-seven and three quarters. I'd made weight, but it took a lot out of me.

When Gacic and I fought the next day, I won the first three rounds easily. Then, in the fourth, I ran out of gas and the bastard nailed me with a good shot to my head—shaking me right down to my fucking toes. Everybody in the auditorium heard the sound from that punch and my mouthpiece ended up in the third row of seats.

As Gacic closed in for the kill, I thought I heard my father's voice say, "Get off the fucking ropes!"

Then I heard him tell me, "Back him up."

I came off the ropes and stopped Gacic's onslaught with a vicious attack of my own. The fight ended up going the distance and I won a unanimous decision.

The next day, I went to see Angelo in his office in the Miami Beach Auditorium, where I'd fought all my fights so far. The walls were adorned with yellowed fight cards, a pair of old boxing gloves autographed by Rocky Marciano, and photos of assorted boxing luminaries. Angelo was seated behind his desk which, as always, was full of papers.

He said, "Oh, here he is now, the next Champ. As long as he keeps his head on straight and doesn't give us any more scares, like he did last night."

Is he talking to me?

I heard a laugh that sounded like my father's. I turned around and there he was; sitting on a couch in the back of the room. As a surprise, Angelo had invited him down to see my first main event. So hearing his voice during the fight hadn't been my imagination and he may have saved me from getting my head handed to me.

Angelo handed me an envelope stuffed with cash and told me I'd fought Gacic like a real champion.

My father and I headed out of Angelo's office into the empty auditorium, and he started to schmooze with me. He told me he thought what I needed was to buy a training camp, and all he needed was a few bucks to hold one he knew about in Derry, New Hampshire. It turned out the "few bucks" was more than the sixteen grand I made from the fight. Like a sap, I handed over every penny to him and said I would tell Angelo to give him my money from the next fight, too.

He said he couldn't have me walking around with no money, so he pulled five hundred dollars out of the money I'd given him and told me to spend it carefully.

I said, "You got it, Pop." He sure did.

Even though I'd "invested" almost all my money with my father, I had enough left to start eating pretty well and that was a problem. I wanted to get a shot at the middleweight title, which meant I had to lose a few pounds. Chuck warned me that if I didn't watch myself I'd never fight in the middleweight division, and would probably be looking at having to go against heavyweights.

* * *

On November 20, 1973, I fought Terry Daniels, who had fought Joe Frazier for the Heavyweight Championship of the World (and went 7 or 8 rounds with him), as well as Floyd Patterson. Terry was six-foot-two and a hundred eighty pounds. I was beating him all the way through, but he hurt me with a right hand in the eighth or ninth round. When that punch landed, the whole place went quiet. But I shook it off and won a unanimous decision.

After the fight, my friend Dick Cami, who owned the Peppermint Lounge and the Top of the Home restaurant in Miami where all the wise guys hung out, said someone special wanted to see me.

"Who is this person," I asked.

"Meyer, Meyer Lansky."

"Who's he and what's so special about him?"

Dick shook his head in disbelief. "Vinnie, he's the guy who really started Las Vegas."

I met Meyer at his hotel, where we drank some champagne and talked. He said, "The way you fought that fight tonight is the same way I do business. I give them a little, give them a little, and they think they are getting a lot. And then I drop the bomb on them. And after I drop the bomb, I know they'll throw things back, but I'm ready and know how to avoid it. That's what you did to that guy in the ring tonight." He treated me to a massage with a four-piece string quartet and Cristal Champagne. What a luxury!

* * *

Sometimes when Angelo was out of town, Chris would put me in with a real comer—someone Angelo wouldn't have wanted me to tangle with that early in my career. Chris used me as a piece of meat though, and as long as he could sell tickets he wasn't concerned about what might happen to me.

In January 1974, he matched me with Baby Boy Rolle. He was one of those really intimidating black fighters, who punched hard and you could hit him with a bazooka and he'd still fire right back at you. In October 1973, he fought World Boxing Council (WBC) Light Heavyweight Champion John Conteh and lost on points after fifteen rounds.

He hit me with a right hand coming out of a clinch and broke my left eardrum. The pain was so severe I thought I was going to die. He knew I was hurt real bad and thought he had me. *Fuck him!*

I fought through the pain and gave Baby Boy all he could handle and more. When the scorecards were tallied after the tenth round, I won a unanimous decision. It was my sixteenth consecutive victory.

* * *

Those were amazing times for me and there was always more excitement whenever Ali was in town. Whenever he spent time at the 5th Street Gym, the place was mobbed with all kinds of celebrities. I saw the president of Panama sitting at ringside with the head of the Medellin drug cartel. The cast and crew of *Miami Vice* were regular visitors. The Beatles even came by one day to see him.

It was a great place to make connections and I made my share.

Chapter Nine

Decisions

With my boxing career really taking off and the victories mounting, I signed a management agreement with the Mendoza Group. The Group was headed by Murray Gaby, a boxer-turned advertising designer, painter, and sculptor. They also managed fighters Marcel Clay, Roberto Ayala, James Scott, and Lou Esa.

When I signed, Murray Gaby took me out for a celebration. We had dinner at the Famous Restaurant. After we ordered I said, "So Murray, why'd you pick this restaurant?"

"Because it's one of the best on the beach."

I smiled. "I know. I've eaten here many times."

He seemed surprised that a guy like me wasn't a stranger to a swanky place like the Famous Restaurant. "You've been here often? I thought you were on tough times until recently."

"Take a walk with me while we're waiting for our food and I'll explain."

I took him around back and pointed to the dumpster. "Over on that end was where they threw the main course leftovers. In the middle was where I slept, and the other end was where they dumped the desserts."

Murray shook his head sadly and said, "All that is behind you, now. Before we're through, you're going to be a champion."

* * *

I had gotten real close to Angelo Dundee and he had become kind of a replacement father figure to me. If I was in a fight and had a bad round he'd tell me, "You're blowing it, Son!"

I'd get so charged up to please him that I'd go out for the next round, take control, and win. I was on a roll, undefeated with seventeen wins, and well on my way to the championship Murray had promised.

On October 25, 1974, I got the chance to put myself into a position to vault to top contender status—a ten round non-title fight against WBC Middleweight Champion Rodrigo Valdéz in Madison Square Garden. Valdéz had won the vacant title that May when he stopped Bennie Briscoe in seven rounds. On September 7, he fought a non-title bout against Cubby Jackson and knocked him out in the second. Now it was my turn to show what I had and that I deserved a title shot.

I was excited, but I was also scared to death. I was only nineteen and was going to be in the fight of my life against a hell of a fighter. Valdéz was a boxer-puncher who could knock you cold with one shot. He was the only guy who ever knocked out Bennie Briscoe. Marvin Hagler couldn't do it and neither could Carlos Monzón—only Valdéz.

And then as the fight date neared, the roof caved in on me. Angelo announced he wouldn't be in my corner—he was going to be in Africa with Ali ahead of the George Foreman fight which was to take place on October 30. Intellectually, I understood his decision, but emotionally I was devastated. Nobody could motivate me like Angelo.

As if that wasn't bad enough, my father showed up in New York for the fight. He was all juiced up seeing my name on the marquis and took all kinds of pictures of it. He tried to act like we were long-time buddies and it sickened me.

Although Angelo wasn't there for the fight, I had the great trainer and cut man Chickie Ferrara and "The Fight Doctor" Ferdie Pacheco working my corner. I gave Valdéz a good tussle and wobbled him a few times, but he beat me by decision. I was disappointed, of course, yet there was a bright side. I went the distance with one of the greatest fighters on the planet at that time.

* * *

Ali's fight with Foreman had cost me Angelo's presence when I fought Valdéz. The only good thing about it for me was that The Rumble in the Jungle got all the headlines and almost nobody was talking about my loss. Even those who were aware of it gave me credit for going the distance with a tiger like Valdéz. Still, knowing that Angelo's main priority was Ali, and not me, made me act crazier than ever.

Angelo and the management team decided to put me to the test. They wanted to see how I handled defeat and if I was worth the effort it would take to make me a champion. Was I going to harness the talent I had and win a title? Or end up as just another whack job hanging around the gym?

Over the next year they put me in the ring with every great fighter they could. On November 26, I fought Chucho Garcia and won a decision. The following February I fought Tony Licata in New Orleans and lost the decision (it was his hometown). At least I got a "Consolation Prize".... Chuck Talhami made me go New Orleans' top rated restaurant, Antoine's. He got back at me a little for all my teasing by telling me, "It's not every day that a Peasant like you gets to eat in a place like this." He was 100% right. Antoine's had been a fixture in New Orleans since 1840, all the stars and Presidents would go there when in town. Anthony Quinn, Farrah Fawcett, Ryan O'Neil were there (not all together). Framed by the exquisite French Antebellum architecture, the food at Antoine's was some of the most delicious food

I had ever eaten in my life, certainly a far, far cry from the leftovers in the dumpster in Miami. Chuck had Filet de Gulf Poisson Almandine, Gulf Fish with toasted almonds and a meunière sauce and I had Crawdad Etouffée, I was in heaven.

* * *

In April I fought Bennie Briscoe to a draw. In August I went to the Tropicana in Las Vegas for a ten rounder against Vito Antuofermo, and lost by decision. In September I fought John Pinney to a draw after ten rounds. After that schedule I figured either Angelo really had a lot of faith in me, or he hated my guts.

I want to tell you the details of the Briscoe and Antuofermo fights.

As the match with Bennie was being setup, he decided that since Angelo was willing to bring his talented white boy to a predominantly black area like Philadelphia, he'd try to intimidate me. For a tune-up fight he went to Venezuela for a bout against Vicente Rondon. I had seen Rondon at the Fifth Street Gym and he was a beast. Bennie knocked him out in eight (this fight isn't reflected on Boxrec.com for some reason). So even though I was happy to get a shot at Bennie, I was psyched out by the Rondon fight and had to force it out of my mind.

During the fight Bennie and I talked to each other. When I landed four great shots to his body he winced. I said, "That hurt, huh?"

Later, he hit me with a powerful left hook and said, "You felt that one, didn't you?"

Yeah, I felt it. I was seeing three of him.

When the round ended I went back to my corner and said, "Angelo, I see three of this fucking guy."

"Don't worry about it. Hit the one in the middle."

In the eighth round he hit me with a left hook that knocked me out. That's right, I was gone. But in a weird turn of events, the right hand he followed with actually woke me up and I made it through the round.

The ninth was even, but in the tenth I went nuts. When the bell rang to start the round, I screamed across the ring, "Bennie! Let's do it!"

I charged at him, backing him up, and pummeling him in his corner and that set the tone for the whole round. We were like two animals trying to kill each other, but when it was over we saluted each other. It took twenty minutes from the final bell until the decision was announced and the fans were on their feet screaming and cheering the entire time. When the draw was announced, Bennie said to me, "You did better than that decision."

For years afterward if anyone tried to get Bennie to say something negative about me, he'd say, "You ain't gonna get me to say anything bad about Vinnie Curto."

The next match was with Vito Antuofermo and, as luck would have it, just when I was starting my training regimen I learned the respiratory illness my father had been suffering from was actually terminal cancer. He had smoked four packs of Pall Malls a day for thirty years. His lungs were filled with blood, and the doctor told him he had forty-eight hours to live. When I went to see him he pulled an article from his wallet about my fight with Valdéz.

I said, "I lost that fight."

He shook his head. "You got robbed."

I went to my training camp and a couple of days later Chuck Talhami pulled me aside and said, "You've got to fight this fight for your father."

"I'll tell you, Chuck, even though I'm still angry with him, seeing him suffering like that was hard for me."

"He stopped suffering at 1:50 this morning."

I took a long walk and then jumped into my car and went for a drive, trying to wrap my head around my father's death and wondering how I should be feeling about it. I turned on the car radio and this song *I'm Not in Love* by the British group 10cc, was playing. The lyrics are: "I'm not in love, so don't forget it, it's just a silly phase I'm going through."

I thought to myself that this is how my father felt, he never could admit to loving anybody. I turned the channel and it was playing the same song! I thought it was just a silly coincidence. I took a deep breath, changed the station once more and there it was again! I interpreted that to mean that from the grave he was telling me that although he couldn't show it, he loved me. Two weeks later I was in the ring with Vito and I dedicated the fight to my father.

Sin City wasn't the best of places for me to spend time before a bout, and I engaged in some things I probably shouldn't have. Even so, I fought a hell of a fight and had Vito on his heels when the final bell rang. He was so sure he'd lost that he left the ring before the decision was announced.

I paced around the ring waiting for the decision, which seemed to be taking forever. Looking back, I think it took so much time because the judges had to change some of their scores to give Vito the win and that's exactly what they did. I found out later that any fight in Vegas in which Vito was left standing, he would be declared the winner.

When I saw Vito afterward he tried to console me. He admitted I won the fight, but said, "Wouldn't you accept it if a decision like that went your way?"

"Yeah, I guess I would."

It's a funny thing with boxers that they can try to destroy each other in the ring and become buddies afterward. That's what happened with Vito and me. We had the utmost respect for each other and became friends.

My next fight after Antuofermo was the draw against John Pinney in Miami Beach. It was another bout I thought I should have won.

I was not happy with the direction my boxing career had taken. I was tired of getting robbed by the judges and felt part of the reason for the bad decisions was Angelo—many in the fight business were jealous of him and some actually hated him. In my mind, that played a role in the Licata, Antuofermo, and Briscoe fights. And I was still stewing about Angelo not being with me when I fought Valdéz.

After the Antuofermo "loss" and the draw against a minor fighter like Pinney, I went to the gym and into a rage. After letting out all my frustrations, I walked out, determined to find another way to earn a living.

Chapter Ten

Another Marriage and a New Promoter

After splitting with Angelo, I returned to Boston. I stopped by my mother's house and my brother Joey was there. I noticed a bruise on his face and asked, "What happened to you?"

"I bought a car from some guy named Dapper and it was a total lemon. When I tried to return it and asked for my money back, he beat me up."

"Oh really? Let's go talk to Dapper and see if he'll reconsider."

When we got to Dapper's car lot, he wasn't there, but his girlfriend was. Her name was Tammy. She was eighteen and gorgeous. She was wearing tight jeans, a halter top, and lots of gold chains. Frankie Valli's *My Eyes Adored You* was playing on the boom box next to her.

"I love this song," she said. "It reminds me of my boyfriend. He's beautiful and here he comes. Ain't he drop-dead gorgeous?"

When Dapper spotted Joey he figured there was going to be trouble and took his sport coat off. Without saying a word I hit him flush in the face with a left hook. Down he went with blood spewing from his nose and lips. That took the fight out of him and he stayed down.

I said to Tammy, "Well, I dropped him. I don't think he's dead, but he sure ain't gorgeous anymore."

To my surprise, she turned on Dapper. "Well, he deserved it for what he did to Joey."

Before we left the car lot, Dapper took Joey's car back and let him pick out a better one for the same price. Almost immediately I started dating Tammy.

* * *

In the meantime, I couldn't get boxing out of my system and went back to the New Garden Gym. Freddie Small had passed away, but I ran into a gangster acquaintance, John "Johnny Gio" Giordano. He was handsome, always well-dressed, and oozed class. He could use his fists, too, and I'd seen him knock guys cold with one punch. Among other things, Gio was a boxing promoter.

He took me to a great Italian restaurant that he owned, and over dinner asked me, "So what happened to Dundee? Did he run out of vicious beasts to put you in with?"

I shrugged. "I was losing decisions or getting draws on fights I should have won. I got tired of getting robbed and figured Angelo was part of the problem. I thought it was time for me to get out."

"Do you mean out of the fight game?"

I shrugged again. "That's what I thought then, but now I don't know. I really miss it and I think I could have made it big. I want to be a champion as bad as I ever wanted anything."

"I believe you, Vinnie, and I think you've got what it takes. Do you want me to get you some fights?"

I made up my mind in a heartbeat. "Yes."

Gio and I became really close and he got me nine fights—eight wins, only one loss, but no knockouts. These were guys I could have knocked out in a couple of rounds but didn't because Gio was betting on the fights. I had to make sure the bouts went the distance so he could win his bets. And the venues I fought in made demands, too. In Rhode Island

I fought a local kid and Gio told me I had to carry the guy to the last round, or we didn't get paid. I did a lot of flashy scoring with nothing on my punches. I tapped him lightly on the chin once and his knees buckled. I actually had to hold him up. It was so obvious it was sickening.

I was making money, though, and without my father around, was able to enjoy it.

* * *

The first time I brought Tammy to Gio's house he stared her up and down without saying a word, and then motioned for me to join him in another room. He said in hushed tones, "Oh my God, she's fucking beautiful. Get her out of here."

A couple of months later we got married. Gio sat next to me at the reception and when one of his fighters named Pete Ricatelli passed by our table, Gio said, "Pete, come here."

After Pete sat down, Gio continued, "I gave you my license to use to open a gym, and two large ($2,000) to cover expenses and my fighters. What did you do? You halfway sold the joint out and what did I get? Not even a thank you. Now, Pete, go think about how you're going to pay me ten grand, which is what I figure you owe me. And if I don't get the ten thousand, you're going to catch a vicious beating. I know you know what that means, a vicious fucking beating."

Pete went off to consider what he'd been told and came back in a few minutes with his answer. "Gio, I gave it some serious thought. I'll take the beating."

Gio and I laughed over that for the next three days and Pete got a pass.

* * *

Tammy wanted to move to Cape Cod so we bought a small house right on the ocean, but she still wasn't happy.

She didn't like me being gone most of the time and said she was lonely, so we started holding parties at our house so she could make friends. After one of the parties, a woman told me she thought Tammy had a bladder infection because she kept running to the bathroom.

When everyone was gone I asked Tammy what was up with the bathroom thing. She said, "Vinnie, at our first party we were all talking and I was doing real well, until one guy started using these long words and I had no idea what they meant. I smiled and tried to say something I thought would work, but when they gave me funny looks I knew I said the wrong thing."

She pulled a little dictionary out of the pocket of her jeans and continued, "So I bought this and now I run to the bathroom and look up the words before I say something stupid and make a fool of myself."

Things weren't going good between us, though, so I moved out and got an apartment in Boston. Our plan was to take a break from each other and then get back together, but the reconciliation never happened.

* * *

Gio set up a match for me against Marvin Hagler for September 24, 1977. At the time, Marvin was just breaking into the top ten, but we knew the fight would be a giant draw locally. We held a press conference to announce the fight. I said what a good guy Marvin was, and how we had worked and trained together at the Petronelli's gym.

When it was Marvin's turn, he said, "When I am in the ring, all I've got on my mind is to destruct and destroy."

It was great psychological warfare on his part and made me feel weak and inferior.

I told Gio I needed to go into a training camp, especially since Marvin was known to use steroids and I couldn't tolerate them. The problem was, Gio was in deep debt from gambling with the big boys and was way behind on his payments—he needed money. The people putting on the fight gave him $25,000 to cover my training expenses, but he used most of it to pay the juice (interest) on his gambling debts. I ended up getting $2,500 to cover sparring partners and facilities.

I should have boxed between sixty and a hundred rounds to get ready for Marvin. Instead, on my shoestring budget, I sparred three rounds with a guy named Mario Rosen in New Jersey. Although he wasn't a bad fighter, it was way too little.

By contrast, Marvin went into training on Cape Cod. He took four sparring partners with him, all of whom were title contenders in their own right.

All this time I was going crazy because I couldn't get my father's words out of my head. What would happen if I blew the Hagler fight and lost my route to a championship? *Would I have to put a gun to my head?*

And then I thought I caught a lucky break. On July 30, 1977, Carlos Monzón successfully defended his title against Rodrigo Valdéz. Monzón retired after the bout, leaving the title vacant.

The WBA and the International Boxing Federation (IBF) got together and proposed a fight between Bennie Briscoe and me in Monte Carlo for the undisputed Middleweight Championship of the world. Out of the blue, my big chance had arrived. There was only one stumbling block—my scheduled fight with Marvin Hagler.

I said to Gio, "Look, I've finally got my shot at a championship. The only thing that can fuck it up is if I lose to Hagler. He's a dangerous guy and I don't want to take the chance by fighting him now. agler Call his people and ask them to let me out of the contract. If I win the championship my first defense will be against Marvin."

Gio said with certainty, "They won't let you out."

It wasn't until later I found out that Gio knew about the proposed fight with Briscoe *before* he made the match with Marvin. But for the championship fight he would not have gotten paid as the promoter. He felt he needed the money more than I needed a title shot.

Still in the dark about what had happened, I wasn't going to give up on getting out of the Hagler fight. I said, "I'm not up for fighting Hagler now. It's too risky and there's too much at stake. How can I do it?"

Gio said, "This is how you do it. You get in the ring and hit the canvass in the first round. You've got the greatest chin in boxing so everyone will think it is a fluke—a lucky punch. Then Marvin gives you a rematch and we sell the arena out again. What do you say?"

"Fuck you," I said, and walked away.

Word that I wanted out of the fight got out quickly and a lot of my fans, Marvin's fans and possibly some gangsters, weren't happy about it. All the major fighters pulled out of fights on occasion, but the backlash to my doing it was horrific.

Four days after I told Gio to fuck himself, I was heading for the gym at the usual time for my daily workout. As I was leaving my apartment building, a friend called to me from his window on the top floor. "Curto, come up. I've got linguine with clam sauce."

I couldn't resist and instead of getting into my car, went back inside. I was enjoying my lunch when I heard a tremendous blast from street level. I looked out the window and there was virtually nothing left of my car—it had been blown apart. Somebody who wasn't happy about the Hagler situation had apparently decided to kill me. If not for my love of linguine and clam sauce I'd have been a dead man. I said to my friend, "I think they're serious."

I knew I had to get out of town until things cooled down. I'd previously met a guy who owned a chain of steakhouses and called him. He said I could hide out at his ranch outside of Seattle, Washington. I called Tammy, who was then pregnant, and told her I was leaving town for a while. I disappeared from Boston and, of course, didn't show up for the Hagler fight. The Boston media went wild.

In Seattle, I got a job cooking and washing dishes in a restaurant. I heard some people from Boston came looking for me, but they didn't find me. I stayed a month or so and then decided that since I was out of the championship picture; I might as well go back to Boston and try to resurrect the Hagler fight.

That was just wishful thinking on my part, though. When I got back, Rip Valenti and the other promoters were so pissed off at me because of all the money they'd lost, they wanted nothing to do with me. What I thought was a lucky break turned out to be a nightmare.

The negative publicity against me ended up helping Marvin. Promoter Bob Arum picked him up and turned him into a big star. As bad as Marvin and the Petronellis talked about me afterward, I believe the non-fight actually helped make Marvin's career.

* * *

A little later on I ran into a promoter whom I had met previously with Gio. His name was Bob Botto, owner of Botto's Sausage and known as The Sausage King. Bob was loaded financially, but even with all his money he had the worst wig in boxing—it looked like he had a dead possum on his head.

He hated Gio and the feeling was mutual. The first time he met Gio and me, he came into the joint we were in with a whore on each arm and said, "I'm Big Bob from the Mob."

Gio said, "You're what?"

"I said I'm Big Bob from the Mob!"

Gio said, "No you ain't," and decked him, sending the possum flying. "Now, you and your whores get out of here."

When I ran into Botto again, we talked about Gio and the Hagler fiasco. He said, "What you need is a real manager. Me."

I didn't have much going for me right then so I thought I'd give Bob a shot. Right away he got me a fight in Upper Darby, Pennsylvania, and followed that up with several more. He was a stingy bastard, though, and wouldn't lay out the money to promote the fights. It was either that or he'd want me to fight real bums so he could bet and make money.

One fight he wanted to set up would have been such an obvious fake that I couldn't handle it. After what happened with Hagler, I didn't want to tell him outright that I didn't want to do the fight. So I set up a stunt at the nightclub Bob owned. One night at closing time, a friend and I hid in the club until everyone was gone, and then we tore the place up a little to make it look like there had been a fight. After that came the funny part.

There was a guy I knew who worked at the morgue and was a pretty shady character. It was rumored that he sometimes helped murderers out by making evidence disappear. He delivered the body of a recent murder victim with a big bullet hole in his head and plenty of blood. We set him up on a stool at the bar like he got killed there.

I called Bob and told him, "Bob, you have to come down to the club. I was driving by and saw the lights on so I stopped. It looks like there's been a fight and there's a dead guy at the bar."

He rushed over and checked out the dead guy. "Who is this guy? Who killed him? How the fuck did this happen?"

"I don't know, but you can't just leave him sitting there."

"A guy killed in my joint and there will be cops all over the place. What a fucking mess this is going to be. They might even yank my license."

"Listen, Bob, if you want to take a chance and keep the cops out of this, I have some friends who might be able to get rid of this guy for you. You'll just have to keep a low profile for a while until we're sure everything is cool."

Bob thought a few seconds and then said, "Okay, do what you've got to do."

"I'll take care of it. Like I said, though, you need to keep out of the limelight. You'd better cancel that fight so you don't have a bunch of reporters hanging around looking for an interview."

"Fight? Oh, yeah, the fight. You're right, I'll call it off. Thanks a lot, Vinnie, I owe you."

The dead guy went back to the morgue for processing and the fight was canceled.

Chapter Eleven

Crossing Sammy "The Bull"

In 1976, I was a sparring partner for future light heavyweight champion Mike Rossman, "The Jewish Bomber." He was a heavy hitter and went through a lot of sparring partners, but when he hooked up with me I was able to take anything he dished out—he didn't need anybody else. Mike's mother was Jewish so he took her name to separate himself from all the Italian fighters out there. His father, Jimmy DePiano, set me up with a part-time job working as a collector for Sammy "The Bull" Gravano.

Jimmy said to me, "Sammy 'The Bull' is looking for someone to go to California for him, see a certain person, and collect some money. I thought of you because I know it's something you can handle and you can use the dough. If you're interested and do a good job, there will be a lot more work for you."

Like most everybody in the Boston-New York area, I knew who Sammy was and had met him a few times. I also knew he was a serious guy—very serious. "What kind of money can I make?" I asked.

"It depends on how much is involved. If the bill is ten grand, you'd get five thousand for bringing it back or just delivering a real strong message that it's past due. If the tab is thirty thousand you'd get fifteen. This California thing is very important and there's some big money involved."

"Where will I meet with Sammy to get my orders?"

"You won't. When it comes to this, I'll be your contact."

"Should I take somebody with me as a backup?"

"It wouldn't hurt, but that's your call. Sammy's deal is with you. If you take somebody along his pay comes out of your end."

I thought it over briefly and then said, "Okay, I'm in."

I took a guy with me on the first job, a big mean-looking bastard who could scare the hell out of anybody just by staring at them. As soon as the deadbeat answered the door I said, "We're from New York and you know what we're here for. This can go easy or hard, it's all up to you."

We must have made quite an impression because the guy's face went white and his legs quivered. After a few seconds he found his tongue.

"I'll have to write you a check, is that okay," he said in a shaky voice.

"Yeah, that's fine," I said. "Just make sure the check is good. If it's not, we'll be back and we won't be happy."

"Wait here while I get my checkbook."

He wrote out a check and handed it to me. "You don't have to worry, it's good," he said.

I smiled. "Thank you. In that case you'll never see us again."

When I turned the check for over seventy thousand dollars over to Jimmy, he was ecstatic. "As soon as this clears I'll give you your money," he said.

Within three days Jimmy paid me over thirty-five thousand in cash and gave me four more jobs. I slipped my helper a few thousand and put the rest in a briefcase—a briefcase that I hoped to fill up.

I was pretty successful in my new sideline and actually enjoyed the work for the most part. However, there were times when it wasn't so much fun, like when I walked into a guy's house and smacked him, then saw his two little boys in their underwear standing behind him and looking really scared.

I quickly said to the guy, "Hey, Buddy, how have you been?" and then I high-fived him. Before I left we chatted pleasantly for a few minutes. Later, the guy paid his debt and thanked me for backing off in front of his kids. He told me that he and the boys started high-fiving each other whenever they had something special to share. Although incidents like this were unpleasant, they were also rare.

Between boxing and collecting, I was knocking down good money and my briefcase was usually full. I would have up to $170,000 in it at any given time.

* * *

Tammy had given birth to our daughter Bianca and I kept in touch with them. In fact, I was still considering getting back together with her. That possibility ended one night when I unexpectedly caught sight of her outside a restaurant after one of my fights. She was getting into a car with a guy and it was pretty obvious from the way they hugged and kissed they were more than friends. What really struck me was the expression on her face—I'd never seen her look so happy.

I called her a couple of days later to discuss our relationship. Because I was doing pretty well financially, I was in a good position to negotiate. Our conversation was friendly and we reached an agreement: I'd sign the house in Cape Cod over to her, give her two thousand dollars a month to help support her and Bianca and give up my parental rights. In return, she'd grant me an uncontested divorce. With my lifestyle I didn't have time to be a father so I agreed and we made our deal.

However, a few months later she hauled me into court looking for more money. The judge told her to go back to

Cape Cod and enjoy her house. The money I was paying her was more than adequate.

That was the end of Tammy and me, although I did find out she remarried and her new husband adopted Bianca.

* * *

In April 1978, Jimmy DePiano told me that Sammy had a favor he wanted me to do for him. He needed a boxer to go up against a New York fighter named Willie Classen in Madison Square Garden and, for whatever reason, Classen had to win. That concerned me because I was still pursuing a title shot and didn't want the loss on my record. Jimmy said not to worry because I could take the fight under an assumed name, so I agreed. I dyed my hair blonde and used the name of Rudy Cruz.

It was a good plan, but as luck would have it the announcer, Jack Granby, recognized me, disregarded what was written on his card, and said, "In this corner we have Vinnie Curto." *Fuck!* Now I was going to get tagged with a loss on my real record. I was screwed.

The bell rang and I went through the motions, giving up every round and drawing boos from the crowd for my lack of effort.

I was in my corner following the third round when I heard cheering. I said to my corner man, "I know that's not for me. What's going on?"

"Frank Sinatra just walked in and the crowd is going nuts."

After the fifth round I had a visitor in my corner: Sinatra's pal and bodyguard Jilly Rizzo. He said, "Frank says he knows a lot about you. You've met and he's seen you fight before. You're better that this and he wants to know what's going on."

I said, "I'm doing a favor for Sammy 'The Bull.'"

"That's about what he thought. Frank said to tell you it's off—go out there and win."

I'd already given Classen five rounds—half of the fight—but maybe I could knock him out or at least salvage a draw. I went out for the sixth and sent Classen reeling from a flurry of crisp punches before we clinched. As Classen and I hugged, I looked out at the audience and my eyes locked with Sammy's, who was at ringside. He was so angry he was foaming at the mouth and screaming, threatening to kill me right in the ring.

Jilly had told me the thing was off, but obviously Sammy wasn't in on that decision. Well, fuck Sammy. I fought the rest of the fight to win.

The fight went the distance and following Granby's announcement of a draw, I knew I was in big trouble and had to get out of there quick. I raced toward the locker room and on the way was intercepted by Jilly and one of Sinatra's other big guys. They accompanied me while I got dressed and then escorted me to their limo for a ride to the Waldorf Astoria, where Sinatra was waiting in a suite on the top floor.

When I walked in the door he was sitting at a big white grand piano, his shirt and tie were open and his soon-to-be-wife Barbara was sitting to his right. He said, "Yeah, it's me. What's going on?"

I told him about my deal with Sammy. He said, "I never liked that guy. I already made a couple of calls and heard Sammy's not happy with you, but don't worry about it. I'm going to take you to Las Vegas with me for safekeeping while I figure out what to do next."

I may not have had Angelo Dundee in my corner any longer, but I now had Old Blue Eyes looking out for me.

Chapter Twelve

François

As promised, Frank Sinatra flew me to Vegas with him. Bob Botto insisted on coming along, too, because he was a huge Sinatra fan and loved Vegas. I said it was okay with me, but that was a mistake. Frank didn't take to him at all and wouldn't even shake his hand, something Bob tried to get him to do several times. I was a different story, though. Frank was always hugging me and he treated me like a king. For the brief time I was with him, everything was first class.

I think the reason Frank was so good to me goes back to when he first became interested in me as a fighter. He checked me out and learned about my childhood. It wasn't commonly known, but Frank was also abused as a kid, himself, and that was our bond. He knew what I'd had to overcome to get as far as I had, because he'd done it, too. When he finally left the world in 1998, he left $5 million for each of his kids, and the rest for abused children.

I'd beat it out of New York in a hurry right after the Classen fight, so I didn't have any personal belongings and very little money with me. One of the first things Frank did when we got to Vegas was to have his drummer, Irving Cutler, take me out and buy me almost five thousand dollars' worth of clothes.

That was generous, but that's the way he was—there was nothing cheap about him. For example, we went to his house in Palm Springs one afternoon with Sammy Davis Jr., Don Rickles, and a famous songwriter (whose name I can't remember) to watch a big football game on TV that night. Everyone wanted hot dogs so Frank sent a guy to the local store, but he brought back a brand Frank hated. No problem. He sent his private jet to Vegas to get the right hot dogs for the game.

One night in 1978, when he was performing at Caesar's Palace, I was backstage with him throwing punches and horsing around while some guys were filming us for a DVD. They wanted me to sign a release form to be included in the film. Frank told me, "One of these days, after six of my friends carry me to my final resting place, that's when this DVD will finally come out and not before." No one believed me when I told that story until about 2006, when the DVD set *Sinatra: Vegas* was released. There I was, in the backstage scenes for nearly twenty minutes. That made me feel like a million bucks.

After a couple of weeks living a great life, Frank said the heat was still on me and I needed to get out of the country while he got things resolved with Gravano. He said he had a friend in Montreal who would take care of me while he ironed things out. So I packed up my new clothes and flew to Canada, leaving Botto in Vegas. There was a small problem, though. The guy Frank told me to see in Montreal wasn't there. He'd gotten into trouble south of the border and was in Leavenworth Prison. However, while I was looking for him I ran into a local gangster named Gaëtan, someone who I'd see plenty more of.

I didn't speak French and that was an obstacle for me in Montreal. Fortunately, Gaëtan told me about a restaurant, Baffone's, where they spoke Italian, which I was fluent enough in to get by. I went there and after mentioning Gaëtan's name, was able to get a job as a dishwasher. Not exactly my dream job, but at least it paid.

Worse yet, the only housing I could find was a room I had to rent from a character named Columbe, a transvestite who thought I was cute. My cost in money was a hundred fifty a month, but I also had to put up with her advances. More than once I'd wake up in the middle of the night to a terrible smell. When I opened my eyes, her face would be right above mine and I'd experience the overwhelming odor of her rotting teeth. We'd usually bump heads as I jumped up in my haste to get away.

It was quite a downfall for a guy who only recently had over a hundred thousand dollars in cash stashed in a briefcase, and then had been part of the entourage of one of the world's greatest entertainers.

* * *

As bad as things had gotten, there was a bright spot. The owner of the restaurant where I worked had a nine-year-old boy, slightly built and very intelligent. I affectionately called him François because he wore a beret all the time to conceal his bald head, but his real name was Joey. I'd often catch him watching me from the kitchen doorway as I washed dishes or peeking at me through the window between the dining room and kitchen. One day I asked his father, Philippe, what was up with Joey.

It turned out there was a big kid at school named Henri, who, with some of his buddies, was torturing the boy, calling him names and pulling the beret off his head and throwing it on the floor. The bullying was impacting Joey's behavior.

I said to Philippe, "Maybe I can train him and teach him how to defend himself." My offer wasn't solely altruistic, only to help François. I was down in the dumps, too, and thought a project like that might benefit me as well.

Philippe said, "Well, Vinnie, I don't know—"

He never got to finish because François, who had been hiding nearby, came running toward us throwing punches and said in rapid fire, "Yes, Vinnie! Teach me! I fight, I train hard, I become fighter!"

I looked at Philippe and he nodded. "Okay, François, I'll train you until you can beat the kid at school. But you're going to have to do exactly what I tell you."

He was ecstatic. "I will, Vinnie, I promise."

After that we talked regularly. François queried me about my life, wanting to know why I did not have a wife and why I was in Montreal. Those talks and his enthusiasm helped lift me out of my depression. But I was having second thoughts about training him. What if things backfired and he got hurt when he confronted the bigger boy? Would I be to blame? With those doubts in my mind, I stalled and dodged François' repeated demands to get started.

Jacqueline, the hostess at the restaurant, was a beautiful girl. She was a long-time friend of Philippe and pretty much ran the restaurant. She was uninhibited and when business was slow she wasn't above turning a trick or two rather than take a paycheck. Still, I was attracted to her.

François noticed the way I looked at her and told me, "Vinnie, you will never have her until you get one thing: love." The kid was wise beyond his years. I was twenty-four years old, yet, at this point in my life I barely wanted to live, let alone love anything.

* * *

It turned out that François and I weren't the only guys with problems. Philippe had his own issues.

One night as the restaurant was closing, I left and was crossing the street when I saw two men go into the restaurant. One of the guys was very large and I recognized him as Gaëtan, the gangster I'd met when I first arrived in Montreal. The other was younger and a little smaller, with a flat nose and a lot of scar tissue on his face. I knew a boxer when I saw one and there was no doubt he'd spent some time in the ring. Based on my experience as a collector for Sammy "The Bull" and what I knew of Gaëtan, I figured they were there on the same kind of mission. Curious, I went to the dining room window and looked inside. Gaëtan and his friend were talking with Philippe, and Jacqueline was standing next to him.

The conversation got animated with Gaëtan jabbing his finger in the air to make a point of some sort. I made up my mind that even though whatever was going on was none of my business, I'd have to go inside and help Philippe if the situation deteriorated.

Suddenly, François burst into the room and started throwing wild punches at Gaëtan. The big man laughed, pushed François away and appeared to say something to Philippe as he did. After that he grabbed Jacqueline firmly by the neck and led her out the door and to his car, with his partner following behind. I could only presume she was helping Philippe pay whatever debt he had incurred. Feeling very sad, I left and went to my room.

The next day I told Philippe I had been watching through the window when his visitors came. "I know it's your personal business, but if you want to talk, I'm here."

He confirmed my assumption that he owed money to Gaëtan and last night's visit was a collection call. Gaëtan's friend, the boxer, was Enzo. When François heard his father being threatened he came to his defense. As Gaëtan pushed him away, he said, "If my men had half of François' heart, I could rule the world." And yes, Jacqueline had paid the interest on Philippe's debt with her body. He didn't provide any details as to why he was in debt to Gaëtan or where François' mother was. Of course I was curious, but I let it drop.

* * *

The bullying at school came to a head one day in gym class. That evening François told his father and me what happened. "I was climbing a rope and Henri shook the rope so hard that I lost my grip and fell. I wasn't hurt and the gym teacher, Mr. Krozie, admonished Henri.

"He then took me aside and said, 'This thing with you and Henri is not getting any better. The worse he treats you the more defiant you become. For that, I admire your courage. But this must stop before you get injured.'

"I told him all I wanted was a chance to take Henri and his friends on, one at a time. After that it will be over."

"Mr. Krozie smiled at me and said, 'Okay, I will schedule a boxing match between you and Henri in two weeks and you will have your chance. If you give a good account of yourself there will be no reason to fight the others. With that, the matter will be finished. If I find out you two have settled the matter elsewhere, I will have you both expelled. I'll explain all this to Henri.'"

I was out of time for stalling. I had two weeks to turn François into a fighter capable of handling a bigger and probably stronger, kid. Still, I had reservations, but they were quickly resolved when Jacqueline, who loved François, asked me to start the training. She said, "If you don't train him, he's going to get into the ring anyway. Don't let him down."

The next day we were at the Olympic Boxing Gym at Park and Bernard. Roger Larivee, a well-known trainer and owner of the gym, came over to us and asked who was going to pay the gym fees for the new student. He also commented on how frail François looked, and wondered if getting into boxing was the right thing for him.

I said, "I'll bet you the gym fees ($20 for two weeks) that my little friend will train for two weeks and win a fight at the end of it." Roger took the bet.

I began François' training by showing him the basic boxing stance. I told him, "This is the foundation of boxing.

It's just as important as having a strong foundation for a house, and without it, you're going nowhere."

For the next several hours Francois practiced his stance until he got it down, and then I showed him how to throw punches, starting with the jab. He was doing very well and I thought maybe—just maybe—we could really pull this thing off.

There were two guys in the ring, one black and one white, who had been doing more arguing than sparring. Their jawing finally got to François. He walked up on the ring apron, stepped inside the ropes and approached the two guys. With his head barely at their stomach level, he said, "I'm sick of listening to you. You're supposed to be fighters, not talk show hosts." I was amazed by the balls the kid had.

At this point, Gaëtan and Enzo entered the gym.

Meanwhile, the two loud-mouths François had scolded apparently realized he was right. They stopped talking and started fighting. I ran into the ring, scooped François up and took him out of the ring and onto the apron.

The white fighter took a hard shot and went down, but sprang back up and delivered a vicious uppercut to the black fighter's chin, sending him to the mat. Three other black fighters who were watching didn't like the way the action was going, and were ready to come to their friend's aid. It looked like things were about to get really ugly.

Suddenly, Gaëtan barked out, "If anyone makes a move to interfere, I will take him down for the count." Everyone froze in place.

I was impressed with the effect Gaëtan's threat had on all those tough guys. It was obvious they knew him and that he'd do what he said. Then, somebody rang the bell and both fighters wobbled to neutral corners, as though they were in an actual prize fight. The place erupted into laughter and even the two woozy boxers joined in. The tension was broken and the danger was over.

Gaëtan noticed François standing on the edge of the ring and went over to him. He said, "Are you here alone?"

François shook his head and then pointed at me, standing a few feet away. Gaëtan recognized me from our previous meeting and motioned me over. This time he eyed me closely, scrutinizing my scar tissue and often-busted nose.

He said, "Are you a fighter?"

I shrugged. "Not anymore."

He didn't press me on it, but I could tell he had something on his mind. François and I left the gym a few minutes later.

* * *

In addition to working in the gym, I began teaching François about running. Road work is critical to being a successful fighter, and my philosophy has always been: If you can't run, don't fight. I didn't try to run him long distances, though, that's for horses. I wanted him to run short distances, but be able to do it consistently.

When we sat down to rest, he asked, "Why did you run?"

I started to explain my theories of training, but he stopped me with, "No, no. I mean this." And then he pulled a folded up piece of paper out of his pocket and handed it to me. It was a newspaper article about the Hagler fiasco that I kept in my room. He must have found it when I took him there to show him where I lived.

That episode brought back a lot of bad memories for me. I said, "I'm sorry, but I really don't want to talk about it."

The nine-year-old boy with the wisdom of a fifty-year-old man, said, "You can run around the world a hundred times, but you will never get away from what is chasing you—it will always be there, eh Vinnie?"

And then he pointed to the top of Mount Royal, where a giant white crucifix towered over the city. He said, "I have run to the top of that mountain many times, Vinnie."

Incredulous, I asked, "You have run up that mountain?"

"Many times," he repeated, "but only in my dreams. And when I get to the top, I feel such peace in my heart. I wish to do it just one time for real."

"Why not just have your father or Jacqueline drive you to the top?"

François smiled. "Yes, I could do that, but I would rather get up there on my own."

I understood where he was coming from and suddenly got all choked up. I gripped his shoulders and told him, "You will, François, we'll do it together."

A day or two later we tried to run to the top of the mountain, but François could only make it half way and we had to stop. We sat down to rest and had a deep conversation. He said, "Will my father come to see me fight Henri?"

"If you want him to be there, I'm sure he will."

He smiled. "Good, that is what I want. Did your father watch you fight?"

I dodged answering and said, "The one person I always wanted to come to my fights as a boy was my grandmother, but she passed away without ever seeing me fight. She was very good to me, though, and I loved her a lot. I'll always remember when she wrapped three gold coins in a white tissue with a gold bow. She handed it to me and said, 'Make three wishes and hold these while you pray to God to give them to you. And then give the coins to someone you love, and their wishes will be granted, too.'"

"Did it work?"

I said sadly, "I don't know because I never tried. Now, I wish I had."

After a few seconds of silence, François said, "I have four wishes. I want to run up this mountain and kiss the cross, I want to fight Henri, and I want my father and mother to reunite."

"The fight is already set up and I promise that before we're finished, you'll make it to the cross. I don't know what to say about your father and mother, but I'll talk with Philippe. That's only three wishes, though. What's the fourth?"

"I can't tell you now, Vinnie. Perhaps someday, but not now."

I was intrigued but didn't push him. We again lapsed into silence. Finally, François said, "I have been thinking about your grandmother. She must have been a great woman for you to love her so much. If I see her before you do, I will give her a kiss for you."

I didn't know what to say, so I said nothing.

The next day I told Francois we'd put off another attempt at running up Mount Royal until after his fight with Henri—with time running out, the fight had to take priority. We trained every day, practicing at the gym and doing roadwork for conditioning. I taught him a special move, where he would jab his left hand up into Henri's face, and then drop down and slam his right hand into Henri's body. I explained to him, "François, Henri is a bully, not a boxer. He'll be confused when you stick your jab in his face. While he's preoccupied with that, you'll pile drive a shot to his body. It will be devastating to an inexperienced kid."

*** *** ***.

I was still very curious about what was really going on with François and Philippe. I wanted to get the whole story and figured if anyone knew what it was, it would be Jacqueline. One day when she and I were alone in the restaurant, I asked if she'd be willing to talk about it. She looked into my eyes for a few seconds, and then said, "Sit down and we'll talk."

She took a deep breath and then began. "I will not talk long because it makes me too sad, but you are one of us now and I think you have a right to know. A few weeks after Joey was born, he was diagnosed with a form of leukemia. His mother didn't want to deal with his illness and left him on a doorstep to become another person's problem. Someone saw her, though, and followed her home with the baby. Philippe went crazy and would barely speak to his wife after that.

"At the time, Philippe owned several restaurants. He took Joey all over the world looking for a cure and eventually sold all of the restaurants except this one in order to pay for Joey's treatments, which were very expensive for Philippe and cost Joey his hair. When all that money was gone and he wasn't able to get a loan from the banks, he went to Gaëtan—there was no other choice.

"Gaëtan comes here every week to collect the interest on the debt. One time when Philippe didn't have the money, Gaëtan said he'd collect from me instead. Philippe told him to go to hell, but I insisted. It happened again the other night, but that is okay. I love Joey with all my heart and there is nothing I won't do for him and Philippe, even that," she concluded, lowering her eyes.

As I listened my emotions ran from sympathy to anger. It was no wonder Philippe seldom smiled, and his expression was usually one of sadness.

* * *

The day of the fight, all the interested kids went to the gymnasium after classes ended, where a boxing ring had been set up. On one side of the ring were all the punks who supported Henri, smirking and laughing. On the opposite side were Jacqueline and other friends of Philippe's. But Philippe, himself, was absent. He was afraid he wouldn't be able to bear it if his son took a beating, so he decided to stay away. François wasn't happy about it, but he said he understood. François then proceeded to point out a woman standing in the back of the room by the exit door. It was his mother, the woman who had tried to leave him on a doorstep years earlier. Apparently she couldn't resist the chance to see what her son was made of.

Mr. Krozie stepped into the ring and made an opening statement. "We come here today to settle the differences between two of our students, Henri and Joey. After this we will study together and laugh together. There will be no more fighting."

I watched the expressions on the faces of Henri and his friends as Mr. Krozie spoke. I wasn't so sure they had any intention of turning into nice guys after the final bell.

François got into the ring and Henri entered a few seconds later. François' training had gone very well and in spite of his lack of size, I arrived at the gym feeling pretty upbeat. When I saw Henri in the flesh, my confidence took a little hit, though. Seeing him and François together was like looking at a boy and a man. I didn't let those thoughts seep into my expression. The last thing François needed was to think I doubted he could win.

Mr. Krozie put the gloves on the fighters and then gave them a few instructions. "No wild swinging and when I tell you to break, stop fighting and step back. If one of you gets hurt, the other one will go to a neutral corner. Now, shake hands and go to your corners."

Henri faked a punch to François' face and Mr. Krozie told him, "Not now. You will have time for that when the bell rings!"

When the gong sounded, Henri strutted cockily across the ring and threw a right hand to François' head—down he went. Henri strolled back to a neutral corner, laughing as his supporters went wild. I jumped into the ring to take François out and stop the fight, but he got to his feet and said, "No, Vinnie! I will fight."

Mr. Krozie said to me, "He wants to continue?"

"Yes, the fight will go on."

Before I left the ring I told François, "He's gonna come at you, swinging wild. Do your thing!"

Mr. Krozie waved the boys back to the center of the ring. Henri strutted, looking out at his adoring fans. Before he knew what happened, François' left jab was in his face, followed by a strong right hand to his ribs—exactly the way we practiced it in the gym.

Henri dropped to the canvass, crying like a baby. The audience and Mr. Krozie were in stunned silence, unable to believe what they'd just seen. I couldn't blame them. I knew it was coming and still it shocked me.

François knelt down next to the fallen bully and put his hand under Henri's head, using his boxing glove as a pillow. Angry, I hollered to him from our corner, "François, get over here. He's the son of a bitch who tortured you. Let him lay there."

"No, Vinnie, the fight is over. We will be friends now."

I thought about it briefly and realized he was right. The kid had class.

When Henri got up he hugged François and then came over to me. He said in heavily-accented English, "You taught Joey to fight like that?"'

I nodded. "Yes, we practiced that move every day in the gym."

"I'd like to train with you one day, and be good in the ring like Joey, not bad in the street like now."

I told him, "Sure, I'll help you."

François won the fight and the bully wanted to change his ways. It had been a fantastic day.

* * *

Following his victory over Henri, François had every right to do a little gloating. He didn't, though. Around the restaurant he was his normal self, as though the fight never happened. However, there was one big change: François' mother began coming around the restaurant. He was very excited when he told me that one night, he saw her and his father dancing in the courtyard after the restaurant closed. He credited me not only with the fight, of course, but with helping reunite them, which I loved. As for Jacqueline, she went to Florida on vacation to escape all the stress and tension.

Two of François' four wishes had come true. We still had to conquer Mount Royal and his fourth wish—whatever it was, though I suspected I knew.

* * *

Gaëtan began to turn up the pressure for repayment of Philippe's loan. In addition to weekly interest payments, he demanded that additional money be paid on the principal.

One day when Gaëtan and Enzo came in for their payment, I observed the scene through the window in the kitchen door. Philippe told Gaëtan he wouldn't have the money for a couple of days. At that, Enzo punched Philippe in the stomach, causing him to double over.

As I was deciding whether to intervene, Jacqueline came running into the room and screamed for the violence to stop. Gaëtan said, "Your womanhood won't help your boss today. Only money will do from now on."

Jacqueline pulled a wad of money out of her bra and handed it to Gaëtan. He counted it and smiled coldly. "This will do until Saturday," he said, "then we'll be back."

The next day I asked Jacqueline and François if we could do lunch together someday. We agreed to do a picnic that weekend at a park with a panoramic view of the city. We ate and talked about pleasant things, with François taking an occasional swig of wine to "wash the cheese down." For the most part it was one of the most beautiful afternoons of my life.

François must have snuck more wine than we saw, and he soon fell asleep. Jacqueline and I went on talking about his wishes and she told me what his fourth wish was. He wanted to see me fight. She explained that I was his idol and he talked about me endlessly.

I looked at the peacefully sleeping boy as she spoke and her words tugged at my heart strings. I had thought surely his fourth wish was to be healed, but instead he simply wished to see me fight. Like her, it had reached the point where there was nothing I wouldn't do when it came to him.

We then talked about our relationship. I told her I liked her very much and was attracted to her, but there were some things about me that were not for discussion. She said, "I understand your need for privacy. Will those things prevent you from letting me get close to you?"

The conversation was becoming uncomfortable for me so I got up and started to walk away. She followed and grabbed me. I kissed her passionately, but when the kiss ended she asked me about Columbe and my living arrangements. Again I was uncomfortable and our moment was gone.

* * *

I needed to go back to Boston for a few days to take care of some business. I kept a very low profile and only saw the people I had to see. I was back in Canada before Sammy or his guys ever knew I had been in the country.

Although I'd only been away a little over a week, when I returned to Montreal I found that Philippe's situation had deteriorated to a dangerous point. He told me François' health had taken an unexpected turn for the worse. The previous night he had stopped breathing and his mother had to perform mouth-to-mouth resuscitation to bring him back. He was hospitalized and the prognosis wasn't good. In addition, Philippe wasn't able to keep up his payments to Gaëtan and the gangster was threatening to take over his restaurant. Extremely depressed and feeling he had no options, Philippe was prepared to put his restaurant to the torch and die in the blaze.

I told him, "I can't do anything about François but pray. The rest is up to the doctors and God. With guys like Gaëtan there is always another way, though. He doesn't really want your business—he wants your money. Let's go talk with him and see what can be done."

Philippe and I went to the Brasserie de Longeville, a cowboy bar Gaëtan owned. He was surprised to see Philippe and me in his office doorway and, suspecting trouble, Enzo took a swing at me. I ducked the punch and flattened him with a combination to the head. Gaëtan stood there with his mouth open, surprised at how easily I disposed of his main man. I said to him, "We didn't come here looking for trouble. We only want to talk."

Regaining his composure, Gaëtan said, "I've checked on you. You're the same Vinnie Curto, the American fighter who could have been a champion, yes?"

I answered, "I could have had a title shot and I believe I would have won."

He smiled and his face took on the look of a businessman with a deal on his mind. "Tell me, Vinnie, are you willing to do a major fight for me?"

"I'll tell you what. I'll do one main event for you to pay off Philippe's entire debt—all one hundred seventy thousand dollars of it. Do we have a deal?"

With almost no hesitation Gaëtan said, "Yes, Vinnie and Philippe, we have a deal."

Chapter Thirteen

Je t'aime

After reaching our agreement, Gaëtan quickly arranged two warm-up fights for me. The first was against a guy named Bill Ramsey on July 17, 1979. I won that bout by a TKO in seven rounds. Twelve days later I fought Jean-Yves Fillion and won a ten-round decision.

The only trouble was that I had no idea who I was warming up for. A smart businessman, Gaëtan wasn't going to let that cat out of the bag until he was good and ready. I had to assume it would be a tough fight and I'd better be in shape. That meant spending a lot of time in the Olympic Boxing Gym.

When I went to the gym to set up a training schedule, I spotted this young kid who was training an amateur boxer. I watched them work and was amazed at how knowledgeable the kid was. It was like there was the mind of a forty-year-old fight veteran in the body of an eighteen-year-old. He knew everything that was important and was able to explain things to his student in easily understandable terms.

While I was watching, Roger Larivee strolled over. He said, "Are you here to get ready for your big fight?"

"How do you know about it?"

He chuckled. "Word gets around."

"Have you heard who I'm fighting?"

"No. Just that it's going to be a big deal here."

It looked like Gaëtan was shrewdly starting a buzz about the fight, but keeping it shrouded in mystery. Good move.

Roger said, "Who do you want to train you?"

I pointed to the kid, who turned out to be Russ Anber. Although he was just starting out then, he went on to become a boxing legend and has worked with seven world champions, including current WBC heavyweight boss Deontay Wilder. Picking Russ to train me was one of the smartest moves I ever made as a boxer. But the thing I most have to thank Russ for was his help with getting my head on straight. I'll talk more about that shortly.

With Russ now in my corner, Gaëtan lined up another tune-up. On August 21, I scored a two-round TKO win over Dennis Waters. After that, information on the main event fight was released and I learned who I was going to square off with: Eddie "Hurricane" Melo, on November 6 at the Forum in Montreal.

* * *

Eddie Melo was a collector for the top gangsters in Montreal. A funny thing about gangsters, they loved to have their top collectors also be top boxers. That tended to make the collection process much easier. In fact, it could sometimes be downright amicable, with autographs and storytelling taking place instead of fists flying.

But Melo was far from being a warm and fuzzy type. As soon as our match was announced he went to work on me in the papers, trying to get inside my head. He knew about my history with my father and told reporters, "He must have liked it."

After two or three articles filled with insults appeared, it was starting to get to me. When I told Russ about it, he nonchalantly said, "Oh, don't worry about it. Go see Rooshi and he'll straighten you out."

"Who in the hell is Rooshi?"

"His full name is Rooshikumar Pondya, Rooshi for short. He's a professor at McGill University (in Montreal) and he teaches people about their EQ."

"EQ?"

"Yeah. You've heard of IQ, haven't you?"

"Sure, that's how intelligent you are."

"Right. Rooshi's deal is Emotional Quotient. It's all about harnessing your emotions. I'll fix you up with an appointment."

Meeting Rooshi would have a profound impact on my life.

* * *

During my visit with Rooshi I bared my past. I told him about my childhood, the abuse by my father and the indifference of my mother. He listened intently and then said, "First, we *must* correct the uncorrected past that lurks in the dungeons of your mind."

He sat me down with a couple of dolls representing my parents. I had long dialogs with them, telling them how I felt. He made me stay with it until I was actually able to forgive my father and tell him I loved him.

From there we moved to the present and Eddie Melo. Rooshi told me to visualize the fight in my mind and how it would go. I talked into a tape recorder over and over as I saw different scenarios, always with me winning, of course.

Next he asked me what I felt about Melo personally, about his taunting and airing my childhood and other problems—like the Hagler situation—in the press. He asked me, "Are you prepared to win?"

"Yes," I answered.

"Are you prepared to love this man?"

I was in a forgiving state of mind, but that was a stretch. I really did want to win, though, and Rooshi made you want to trust him.

I said, "Yes," and when I did I felt a rush of power and a surge of confidence that I would win the fight.

I left Rooshi feeling better about myself than I had in a long time. And then the roof fell in. Gaëtan was going to bet a lot of money on Melo. To payoff Philippe's debt, I would have to throw the fight.

* * *.

I was torn. It was one thing to carry a guy for a few rounds, but to intentionally lose to a somebody like Melo went against everything I believed in—especially when there was no doubt in my mind that the fight was mine for the taking. I *knew* he couldn't beat me.

Gaëtan took me to another French cowboy bar to show me off and get more attention for the upcoming fight. Little English was spoken and the music playing on the jukebox was all in French. I went through the motions of meeting people while I privately prayed for a sign showing me what to do. I even asked my father for guidance.

Suddenly, a song in English started playing. It was *I'm Not in Love* by 10cc, the same song that seemed to be playing on every radio station the day my father died. There was my sign. I was going to fight to win and put the rest in God's hands.

I was sitting next to another Montreal gangster named Eugene. He asked me, "So, Vinnie, who should I bet on for the fight?"

Here was my chance to send a message that would certainly get back to Gaëtan. I said, "Eugene, I'm going to win. Bet your house on me and tell everyone you know to do the same."

* * *

Melo and I each had final warm-up fights on the same card at the Forum in Montreal, on October 2. I fought an eight-rounder against one of the toughest guys in Montreal, Marciano Bernardi. It took a gargantuan effort on my part to get a unanimous decision. Melo took on a mediocre fighter named Al Perez and easily knocked him out.

In the weeks between then and the Melo match I studied films of his fights. I noticed in each bout he would come from his dressing room, jump over the top rope into the ring, and go directly to his opponent's corner, push him and scream at him. At the pre-fight press conference I told him, "If you come at me before the opening bell like you usually do, I'll pick you up and bounce you on your head; the fight will start and end right there."

The night of the fight I was in my dressing room when suddenly in walked a blast from the past: Johnny Gio. I didn't know the fight had attracted interest in the States, but apparently it had. He had a guy called "Turk" with him and wanted to make sure I understood they, too, expected me to lose.

Gio said, "Vinnie, you're going to take it easy tonight, right?"

"Wrong. I'm going to give this guy a beating."

"That wouldn't be wise. We heard the smart money up here was going on Melo and that it was a sure thing. Some of us bet that way and we want to make sure you don't pull the same thing you did on Sammy (Gravano)."

"I told you I'm going to win. If you bet wrong, that's on you."

At that point Russ came in, followed by Eugene—all three hundred fifty pounds of him—Claude Faber, another huge gangster, and Montreal's big boss, Frank Cotroni. Eugene said, "Vinnie, you have a fight to warm up for."

"That's right," Cotroni said to Gio and Turk. "Gentlemen, let's get out of here so Vinnie can go about his business. Come and watch the fight with us."

Gio was smart enough not to argue.

*　*　*

I had a small contingent at ringside to cheer me on. Rooshi was there, along with Philippe Jacqueline, and François. I was tickled to be able to fulfill François' wish to see me fight but, by this point, he was so weak I tried to talk him out of coming, but he wouldn't hear of it.

After I entered the ring, Melo came down from his dressing room to the theme song from *2001, A Space Odyssey*. He jumped over the ropes as always but stayed in his own corner. I said to Russ, "It looks like we put the fear of God into him."

He laughed. "Yes, we did."

When the bell rang, Melo came out smoking. I stood right in front of him and made him miss again and again. I knew that would get him frustrated and make him even wilder. Then I'd tie him up, walk him back, and let him go. He didn't change strategy and kept coming back at me. After a couple of rounds, instead of clinching, I began throwing crisp combinations when he charged and made him pay for his misses.

And then, of all things, my corner ran out of water. Rather than tell me about the mistake, Russ said, "You don't deserve any water for that round. Get back out there and really work for it."

I went out and had a fantastic round. By the time I got back to my corner Russ had stocked up on water.

I pitched a shutout over the last four rounds. Seven, eight, nine, and ten were all mine; and I nearly knocked Melo out in the tenth. I won a unanimous decision.

I was in my dressing room singing Sinatra's *My Way*, when a guy from the Forum came in with a telegram from Sinatra. He congratulated me on my win and said he had everything straightened out for me back in the States—I could return in safety whenever I wanted. That was welcome news, but I had to acknowledge that had I not been exiled I would never have met François and so many other great people.

My elation was short-lived, though. That same evening I received a message from Jacqueline stating that François wasn't able to breathe and Philippe and his wife had taken him to the hospital. She was waiting outside to drive me there.

When I saw François I said, "François, please hold on. We're going to get you well, don't give up!"

He said, weakly, "No, Vinnie. Last night I had a talk with God, he is going to take me to a higher level now."

I realized this was my last chance to give him his other wish—to go to the top of Mount Royal. I asked his parents if I could take him there and they agreed. Borrowing Philippe's car, I drove to the base of Mount Royal and parked. François was going to run up that mountain, even if it was on my legs. I took him in my arms and up we went.

When we reached the top, the cross was bathed in moonlight. I saw François' beautiful face break into a smile. After kissing the base of the cross, he kept staring at it and said, "Vinnie, I see your grandmother. She is so beautiful, with her long hair almost down to her ankles. She's smiling at us, Vinnie."

I had never described her to him, but she did have very long hair that extended well below her waist. François turned his face back toward me and then I felt him go limp. I knew his soul had left his body and ascended to heaven. I screamed at the top of my lungs for all of Montreal to hear, "He made it! He made it!"

The French term for "I love you" is *Je t'aime*. In only nine years, François had lived a full life and changed the lives of those around him for the better. He taught me the true meaning of love.

François, *je t'aime*.

Chapter Fourteen

Canadian Sunset

The next time I saw Gaëtan was at François' funeral. I was standing next to Philippe's chair in the receiving line and was very apprehensive as Gaëtan walked up to us. And then he smiled slightly and said to me, "Vinnie, I knew you were going to fight Melo to win—you told everybody you were going to beat him. Hey, I wouldn't want to lose to that guy either. Anyway, I believed what you were saying and put my money on you. The odds weren't as good as on Melo, but I still made a ton. We are friends, you and me."

He then looked at François' frail body in the coffin and said sadly, "I had no idea what Philippe needed all that money for. Now I know."

Gaëtan nodded to a man standing near the entry door. The guy came over and sat two satchels on the floor next to Philippe, who stared at Gaëtan in confusion.

Gaëtan leaned toward Philippe and said in a voice just above a whisper, "I should not have taken your money under those circumstances. Consider what I loaned you as a gift and what is in those bags will help get you back on your feet."

When Gaëtan moved on, another gangster named Michel Marion was next in line. I had met him a couple of times and he was known as a stone cold killer. Yet, when he looked at François in the casket, he showed a soft side. Michel said to me, "I never had any kids, but if I had a son I think I would want him to be like this one."

"You couldn't do any better," I said.

That evening when Philippe opened the satchels, he was shocked at Gaëtan's generosity. They contained enough money to pay off his bills and perform the upgrades necessary to turn his restaurant into one of the best in Montreal.

I didn't have any further dealings with Eddie Melo. However, he continued to live the Mob life and was shot to death in an underworld hit in Mississauga, Canada, in April 2001. His daughter and I have become friends through Facebook and are helping kids in the area today through her organization, the Eddie Melo Foundation.

* * *

Sinatra had cleared my path back to the States, and with François gone and my relationship with Jacqueline going nowhere, I figured it was time for me to leave.

I wanted to pick up a little extra cash first, though, so I stayed in Montreal and fought one more fight. On January 20, 1980, I knocked out a guy named Kelly Anderson in three rounds. However, that bout wasn't nearly as exciting as what happened on January 18, two days before the fight.

I was up in Sainte-Adèle, at Le Feu de Bois restaurant with Claude Faber, Frank Cotroni, and Gaëtan. Michel Marion came in and sat at a different table. Michel was my good friend for almost the entire time I was in Montreal. Even though I grew up in Boston and he in Montreal, we felt like brothers. Michel even told me secretly one day he thought that perhaps we might have been brothers in another life. I knew something was off, however, the time he told me, "Vinnie, there may be a time when you don't love me anymore."

"Never," I said.

He replied, "If that ever happens, don't worry about it. Wherever I am, I'll understand."

I thought he meant he might have to leave Canada.

Little did I know at the time, but there was a ski resort owned by Yves Charlebois. Yves used to bring the homeless, the poor, the sick, and Jerry's Kids, to his resort and give them lunch and all the rides—it was the greatest thing. Sometimes a poor family would get evicted and come to Yves' hotel and ask how much for one night. He would say, "For one night? You need to stay the whole week for nothing."

Usually, all the businesses had to pay the Mob bosses for protection, but Cotroni felt Yves was a saint, and told him he would never pay a penny again. He told all the wise guys, including Michel, "Don't touch this guy. *Not ever.*"

That came about because Cotroni had tried unsuccessfully to get a room at the resort and was upset. Yves brought him there and showed him the rooms were all filled with the sickly and the poverty stricken. Cotroni had a big heart for things like that and ordered that Yves be left alone. But Michel, addicted to the money, kept collecting it from Yves and some of Cotroni's other off-limits people. When Cotroni found out, he became enraged and warned Michel to stop. "Stay away from Yves. He is not to be bothered."

His additional warning fell on deaf ears.

Cotroni had no tolerance when it came to disobedience. When he found out Michel had continued to collect protection money from Yves, he felt he had no choice but to make an example of him. The situation became even more sinister when Michel, fearing Yves would complain to Cotroni, murdered Yves to seal his lips. Michel's actions sealed his own fate. To old-school gangsters like Cotroni, when you do something really wrong, you're a dead man. That's the way it had to be. But I knew none of this when I went to the restaurant that day.

Michel was barely in his chair at Le Feu before Cotroni got up and left. He returned in about ten minutes and whispered something to Gaëtan, who nodded. We sat there talking for several minutes and then I said to Gaëtan, "I think I'll go over and say hello to Michel."

As I started to get up, Gaëtan put his hand on my leg to stop me. He shook his head and said, "Not now. Stay here with me." I had no way of knowing what, but I knew something was definitely up.

Within seconds a skinny guy came in and walked toward Michel. He said, "Michel Marion?"

Michel turned toward him and smiled, "Oui," he said, without hesitation. The man pulled a revolver out of his waistband and fired two shots. Michel went down, his body quivering. The guy stood over him and fired another round into his head—the quivering stopped.

Like nearly everyone else in the restaurant, I sat there in shock. Two people who didn't seem surprised, though, were Frank Cotroni and Gaëtan. I found out later they knew it was coming because the killer, Réal Simard, was Frank Cotroni's driver, bodyguard, and hit man.

I was so sad, and crying uncontrollably, Cotroni had to level with me. He told me about Yves and that Michel had killed him out of fear he would complain that Michel was still extorting him. Cotroni said, "You catch him on a bad day, he could have killed you, too."

Now, seeing Michel for what he really was, I facetiously asked Cotroni, "Is there any way I can resurrect him, so I can kill him myself?" They loved me for that.

I was devastated, though, thinking of all the people Yves used to help and wondering what would happen to them with him gone. At the funeral, I met his son, who was just as beautiful as his dad and had even more heart. He picked up right where his father left off, but with a little more smarts when it came to finances.

The best thing of all is Yves comes to me at night sometimes, just like my mother. When I try to tell him I'm sorry—that I wish I had known what was going to happen and could have prevented it. He tells me, "No, don't worry, it's all perfect. You will see one day."

The sun had set on the Canadian portion of my life. My next stop was another return to Boston.

* * *

Johnny Gio heard I was back in town and reached out to me. He said he wanted to make peace with me and had a deal that would benefit both of us. I was still under contract with him and he wanted to sell my contract to a guy he owed money to. That would square Gio's debt and the new guy would be able to get me some decent fights. I told Gio that was fine with me and to go for it. It turned out to be a good move, because after two lesser fights I got a chance to fight Bennie Briscoe again on December 15, 1980—this time in Boston. I beat him over ten rounds and this time they gave me a unanimous decision.

I won a few more fights in New England and Gio introduced me to a couple more characters, one of whom was Johnny "Turnstile" Dunn. The guy was part of what was called "The Tomato Can Crew," that arranged for fighters willing to lose to go up against comers that needed to build a record. No matter whether the fight was amateur or professional, Johnny provided the losers. And the more the money, the better his fighter's acting ability would be.

Dunn got his nickname because when he said something really positive about a guy, if whoever he was speaking with disagreed, he'd turn on a dime and go negative, or vice versa.

Let me give you an example: Dunn would say, "Vinnie Curto is a solid guy."

If the listener said, "I don't think so. I hear he's got head problems."

Dunn would come back with, "You're right. He's all fucked up and he's no fucking good."

When Dunn got subpoenaed to testify at a racketeering trial, he ended getting indicted himself, on 136 counts of perjury for refuting his own testimony.

* * *

I've talked about the seedy side of boxing and some of the things I was personally involved with—like carrying opponents for extra rounds or letting them win. I've also mentioned the likes of Gio and Johnny Dunn. Before I move on I want to make something perfectly clear to you, though: we, myself and the acquaintances I've told you about, weren't the only people involved with shady deals in the fight game.

The whole time I was fighting, organized crime and illegal activities were part of the boxing business. Fixed fights, illegal betting, and crooked judges were the norm. I believe my refusal to go as far into the gutter as some people wanted is a major reason why I didn't get the title shots I should have had. I wasn't great when it came to the "political side" of the business and didn't have promoters powerful enough to back me. Those shortcomings cost me and I paid the price. I'm not crying about it, though, I'm just explaining the nature of the fight game when I was in it.

I did have some powerful friends that weren't directly involved with boxing, though. Let me tell you about a guy named Sal, an organized crime boss in the Bronx. After a fight arranged by a well-known black promoter, I got a threatening letter from the IRS stating that I owed a huge tax bill. I was looking at up to five years in prison if I didn't straighten things out. I met with my lawyer and he said I'd have to have earned a million dollars to owe the amount of tax the IRS said I owed. I didn't know who got that money, but it sure as hell wasn't me.

I called the promoter, one of the most well-known in the world, but I won't mention his name, to tell him there'd been a mistake in my earnings he reported to the IRS and he needed to correct the number. I was more or less told to go fuck myself so I reached out to Sal.

We met at his favorite Italian restaurant. Sal told me I had to try the veal, but I said, "Sal, I'm looking at five years in the pen and I'm too upset to eat. I'll just have coffee."

Sal said reassuringly, "Don't worry, Vinnie, I'm sure it's nothing we can't handle. Tell me about it."

I explained my situation and Sal interrupted on occasion with a question. When we were finished he said, "Okay, let me see what I can do. I want you to come back here tomorrow afternoon at two o'clock and we'll talk some more. Have the scallopini! The scallopini, I'm telling you buddy! If you get this to the judge, you'll get a suspended sentence." I told him if he was able to straighten this out, I might be able to eat.

I got to the restaurant the next day and had just sat down at Sal's table when the promoter showed up. He nodded to me, sat down, and said, "Sal, what did you want to see me about?"

Sal said, "You put all that money on Vinnie's social security number and caused him a lot of headaches. Now it's your headache. You're going to pay his fucking tax bill and you're going to pay it *now*. Tell Vinnie's lawyer as soon as it's done"

Then Sal turned to me. "Vinnie, if this fucking prick doesn't pay you call me immediately, understand?"

I nodded.

The expression on the promoter's face said he knew he was in deep shit. I gave him my lawyer's info and then he excused himself with an "I'm sorry this happened."

I called my lawyer and told him I might escape this certain doom, but I wasn't feeling like it. Two days later he called me and said, "Not only did your tax bill get paid, they reimbursed you for what you already paid me. I've got your check here at the office."

The old saying that it isn't what you know but who you know, was sure true that time.

My next big adventure took me a long way from Boston and it almost cost me my life.

Chapter Fifteen

Thailand—A Trip to Die For

In 1982, an attorney representing the Royal Thai Consulate in Boston contacted me about a very serious problem—all the consulate files had been stolen from his office. It happened he knew the identity of the thief. He also knew that any publicity about the missing files would probably cause serious damage to his practice. Because of that he didn't want to involve the cops and was looking for non-law enforcement assistance.

I asked the lawyer what was behind the theft, what benefit were the files to the thief?

He explained that the guy who stole the files worked in the consulate's office. He had come to him with a case he wanted the lawyer to take, which would have involved concealing evidence. The lawyer turned him down and the guy wasn't happy. He stole the files to punish the lawyer, by embarrassing him and hoping to ruin his business. The lawyer and the Thai Consulate would be very grateful to anyone who could recover the files without publicly exposing the episode. I told the lawyer I'd think it over and get back to him.

I next reached out to a couple of mid-level wise guys, explained the situation to them and came up with a plan. We'd recover the files and convince the thief not to cause any further problems. Rather than ask for a direct payment, our compensation would come in the form of a big money fight for me in Thailand—a million dollars—set up by the Thai government. I gave the lawyer the proposal and he accepted it within a couple of days.

My friends and I scooped up the thief and took him for a ride. We told him in detail what would happen to him if the files weren't returned immediately or if he continued to cause trouble. We got his attention and between sobs he agreed to get the files back to the lawyer that same day and then disappear.

The lawyer and his clients were ecstatic. They had their property back and nobody was the wiser. Now it was time for them to pay their debt. I prepared to head for Thailand and a big payday against an opponent to be named later. I'd get an advance from the promoter upon my arrival; do a tune up fight and then a main event. It was a good plan, but things don't always work out as we hope.

* * *

When I first arrived in Bangkok I noticed the smell of raw sewage and barbeque fuel. I was told that hibachis were a main heat source for preparing meals and there were over nine million of them in the country. Not many people had food, but they all seemed to have hibachis.

I hooked up with a guide named Chai who showed me around. As we left the tourist areas, the smells and visuals struck me like a hook to my jaw. The worst part was the kids with swollen stomachs and their hands clenched in misery. *What kind of place is this?*

There were a lot of newspapers there which were sold at sidewalk newsstands. As I walked the streets, I was amazed to see my picture on almost every newspaper. An American coming to Thailand for a fight was big news.

I got a thousand dollar advance from the fight promoter and needed three suitcases to carry what I thought was a rather measly amount of cash in baht, the monetary unit of Thailand. However, in Thailand that kind of money made me a rich man. All the bills had a picture of the Queen of Thailand on them and as I looked at her, I thought of all the starving and sick children I'd seen. I wondered how she could live in luxury while all that suffering was going on around her.

Maybe the rulers of the country weren't concerned, but I was. I told Chai, "I want to help the kids. What's the best way to do it?"

"Don't give them any money because the adults would take it from them. Buy them food and stay with them while they eat."

We went to one of the floating markets where I bought two small boats and loaded them up with food. We then transported everything to the poorest neighborhoods and started feeding the children. I was a hero temporarily, but that quickly changed because in their weakened condition the food was too much for them—they got even sicker and two of them died over the next few hours. At first I didn't know what was happening, just that people were screaming and something was wrong.

After a couple of minutes I realized what had gone down. That was bad enough, but then a Thai newspaper reporter came up to me and asked in broken English, "Why you kill the kids?"

That was it. I lost my cool and shot my mouth off in a rant. I screamed at him, "Your king and queen killed those kids. That fucking money-mongering queen of yours sits in her palace while the children starve."

Chai tried to shut me up, but I shrugged him off and kept yelling at the reporter. "Did you hear me? I said your queen is a no good bitch. Fuck her!"

After I calmed down and the reporter left, Chai told me I had to stop worrying about the kids and how they lived. That was the way it was and nothing I could do would change it. He warned me that publicly disrespecting the king and queen could put me in great danger. "This isn't the United States, you know. We do things differently here."

It turned out that it was already too late for that, though, and when my tirade hit the papers it offended some very important people.

* * *

I pushed the kids and their plight out of my mind and started training. I still envisioned doing a tune-up fight and then taking on my still unnamed foe in the big event. Even though I didn't yet know his identity, I had to assume they weren't going to pay me the big money to fight a bum, so I knew I'd better be ready.

One day after training, one of the Thai fighters I was working with said in his broken English, "Vinnie, you need good massage."

I couldn't argue with that. My muscles ached and the thought of getting rid of the pain and stress appealed to me. I said, "That sounds great. Do you know somebody?"

He smiled. "I take you to guy who have number one girl. She very good."

We walked from downtown Bangkok to Patpong, the red light district. I knew then that this wasn't going to be a simple massage, but I was up for some action and continued on.

The kid led me into a building where a really skinny Thai guy was. His head was big and round, with long hair on the sides and a receding hairline. He wore suit pants with suspenders and stood there holding a cigarette as he stared at me.

After a few seconds a devious smile slowly spread across his face and he said to me, "I have something very special for you. You number one, she number one."

I looked at the kid who brought me. He said, "Di Mach ma!" I knew that meant I was going to have something very good and beautiful. Then the kid left me alone with the pimp. He said, "You give me five hundred baht (Thai currency with one baht equaling about twenty-five cents US) for number one girl?"

I said, "Four hundred-fifty baht."

He stepped real close to me and said through rotten teeth, "You smart man. You want number one girl you have to pay five hundred baht."

His breath was so horrible I almost fell to my knees. I agreed to his price just to get him away from me. He smiled and said, "You come this way."

I followed the pimp to a small room with a bed, bathtub, and towels. I sat on the edge of the bed for about five minutes until two young boys and a young girl came in—I doubt if any of them were over ten years old. They came to the foot of the bed and the boys stared at me while the girl stood with her head bowed. Nobody spoke. We remained that way for a few minutes and then I said to the kids, "Go get your uncle, father, or whoever that guy is. I'm expecting company and nobody has come yet."

The kids left and a couple minutes later they were back along with the pimp. He said a couple of words to them in Thai that I didn't understand, and they turned very serious. The boys remained motionless and the girl began unbuttoning her blouse.

I finally realized that this child was the pimp's number one girl—the "company" I'd been waiting for. No world champion boxer could have hit me any harder than that reality. I went to the girl and buttoned her blouse up. When I did, she went limp, but I didn't know whether it was from fear or relief.

I said to the pimp, "I want to make sure I understand this. Where is the number one girl you promised me?"

He smirked, walked over to the little girl and slapped her across the face as he hissed a couple of words to her. She started to undress, again. The smirk on the pimp's face only lasted until my left hook landed on his chin. When he dropped to the floor I started kicking his oversized head. The little girl started throwing punches at me and hollered for me to stop. I didn't, though. I kept on kicking until the pimp was unconscious. I then picked the girl up. She was still crying and screaming, but calmed down quickly and wrapped her arms around my neck.

I knew that when the pimp came to he'd want revenge on me and maybe the kids, too. Carrying the girl, I told the boys to follow us to the street. I flagged down the first cab I saw that was big enough for all four of us and told the driver, "Just drive out of this area. I'll tell you where to drop us after we've driven a while."

When we were clear of Patpong I told the driver to stop so I could make a phone call. I got hold of Chai and explained what had happened. I finished with, "I'm going to take the kids to the American Embassy. I'm sure they'll be able to help."

There was dead silence on the phone for several seconds, and then Chai said, "As you wish."

I knew that meant he didn't agree with me, but rather than argue about it he'd let me find out for myself. *So be it*.

When I got to the American Embassy I told the clerk I needed to speak with a representative. After a surprisingly short wait, a man came out and took us into an empty office where I explained the whole situation.

He listened politely and his answer was short and to the point. He said, "I sympathize with your situation and admire what you're trying to do. But look at it from my perspective. You go into a cesspool like that expecting to find what, a Garden of Eden? America contributes enough money to this place and we're not going to start taking care of local kids who are having it tough—that's a problem for the Thai government to deal with. I'm sorry, but that's the way it is. You're on your own."

I told the guy what I thought of him, took the kids and left. We hailed another cab, drove around for a while and then I called Chai to meet us at a restaurant in Siam Square. Although he'd been right about my visit to the Embassy, to his credit he never once said "I told you so."

* * *

Chai told me of a place near Chang Mai (a city nearly 400 miles from Bangkok) where kids from broken homes or who were being abused could go and be safe. I took the money I had left, rented a big Japanese car, loaded the kids and Chai and headed for what I hoped was a safe haven. The kids loved the car and riding that distance in it was a real thrill for them, making for a pleasant trip.

We arrived at what I called the "children's ranch" early in the morning and the first thing I noticed was the absence of the stench that engulfed the poor areas around Bangkok. I left the kids in the car and entered the main building. It was like a dormitory and I saw several small children making their beds and joking with each other. I next looked into the kitchen where other children were cooking breakfast while adult supervisors looked on. All the kids looked healthy and acted happy—a far cry from the conditions we'd come from. I knew my three refugees had found a home.

Chai made the necessary arrangements with the people running the place and I handed over the rest of my money. Just as we were getting into the car to leave, my "number one girl" came running over. She jumped into my arms, hugging and squeezing me tight. After several seconds she stepped back, smiled, waved and ran back into the house. I was broke but seeing that smile—the kind of smile you *should* see on a child's face—was worth any price. Satisfied,

I got behind the wheel and Chai and I started the long ride back to Bangkok and my big payday.

* * *

I moved out of my hotel and into a mosquito-infested training camp where the Thai fighters trained. Almost immediately the newspaper reporters caught up with me, wanting to know what had led me to take up residence in such a primitive environment.

Still upset, I said, "I'd love to see the king and queen spend one hour sleeping in this room. Maybe then they'd understand how fifty percent of the people in Bangkok live. I think they already know, and they just don't care."

The reporters ate it up and the next day my comments were on the front page of most of the newspapers. Two days after that some guys came to the gym, started talking with the Thai fighters, and then got close to me. When my workout was over, they asked me if I'd like to go drink a few beers. I agreed.

They took me to this small shithouse of a place in Patpong. There were female impersonators all over the place and I was downing a lot of beer. I remember after a trip to the men's room my beer had a funny taste, but by then I didn't really care. A little later one of my new "friends" said, "Let's get out of here and go to another club where there are real broads."

We jumped in the car and started driving. We hadn't gone very far when I started hallucinating—I thought the buildings we were passing were melting. I was sweating profusely and very dizzy. Through the fog I knew somebody had slipped something into my beer—I'd been drugged.

I was in the front seat and I felt hands all over me as the guys in the back were searching me and taking my identification. I knew it, but I couldn't do anything about it.

I was totally helpless and unable to move. *They're taking me somewhere to kill me. I've got to do something!*

The fear that gripped me gave me strength and I did the only thing I could do—I attacked the driver. I hit him in the face as hard as I could. He lost control of the car and we crashed through a fence and slammed into a statue of Buddha. I crawled out of the car and tried to walk, but my legs were numb, and I fell down. That was the last thing I remember of what happened at the scene.

My next memory was looking down from the ceiling of a room at a gurney with people in medical garb standing around it. They were working on somebody who was dying. They were working on me. I screamed, "I'm alive! Do you hear me, I'm alive!" They didn't hear me and not a single head turned up toward me

Confused, I looked behind me and saw an incredibly bright light. I knew the light was good and if I could get to it I'd be safe. But when I tried to move toward it I was stopped by a force I couldn't see.

I looked back down into the room as a guy in a military uniform stepped to the gurney. He slapped my face a couple of times and then put a sheet over my head. *Maybe I'm dead after all.*

Seconds later another guy entered the room and said something to the doctor. The doctor then removed the sheet and inserted a needle into my heart. Next I heard a loud noise and was back inside my body. I opened my eyes and they were all there, the doctor and his assistants, the military guy and the stranger. I was later told I had enough number four heroin in me to kill a herd of elephants.

I believe I was targeted by the Thai military because of my comments about the king and queen. Had the military guy in the hospital had his way, I'd have been flown back to the States in a box instead of going under my own power. Needless to say, there was no fight and no payday. However, I was still alive.

* * *

I "died" thirty-four years ago and am still searching for the reason I was spared. Every day I am still breathing is purely a gift from a Higher Power, and I try to give back all I can. Although I'm very, very far from being wealthy, I go out of my way to help people I don't even know because I believe it's what He wants me to do.

If this book is successful or one of my other endeavors comes through, I'll be able to do a little more for others and maybe something for myself. You see, I dream of going back to Thailand and see that little girl as an adult, probably with a family of her own. No matter how much she may have changed, I'm sure I'd recognize her beautiful smile.

Yes, I died in Thailand, but in death I was born.

Chapter Sixteen

Sly Stallone and My Time at Mustang Ranch

After my Thailand adventure, I returned to Boston. I met a girl there—she was a real knockout and I couldn't get enough of her—and we flew down to Miami for a week. Naturally, I stopped in at the Fifth Street Gym.

Richie Giachetti, who trained heavyweight champion Larry Holmes and later Mike Tyson, came running up to me. He said, "Vinnie, am I glad to see you! Lee Canalito is signed for a $25,000 fight and he just got his nose broken and can't do the fight. Can you take his place? Are you in shape?"

Canalito was a heavyweight known as the "Italian Stallion" and was managed by movie star Sylvester "Sly" Stallone, who played fighter Rocky Balboa in a series of boxing films.

"Yeah, Richie, I'm in shape," I laughed, "but I'd take the fight even if I wasn't."

Richie was ecstatic. He got right on the phone and called Stallone. He said excitedly, "Sly, we got Vinnie Curto!" Richie then passed the phone to me.

Sly said, "Vinnie, I really appreciate you taking this fight. If you do it under my promotion company, Tiger Eye Productions, I'll get you a bunch more fights, maybe even a title shot."

My first fight for Sly was on September 9, 1982, against a guy named Hector Negrete. When I looked up his record there was a five-year gap. When I met Hector before the fight I said, "What were you doing for those five years?"

"Five years," he answered.

I won the fight by unanimous decision.

For my next fight Sly matched me with Jeff McCall, a more experienced fighter and a much better puncher that Negrete, at Caesars Palace in Las Vegas. It was going to be a big TV fight broadcast on ESPN. Sly wanted me to be in top condition and I really appreciated him wanting me to help get me in shape.

During training I moved into Sly's home on Amalfi Drive in Pacific Palisades. His training methods were unorthodox, to say the least.

I'll always remember doing the crazy "chase the chicken around the pool" routine he had me do with a fighting gamecock worth $30,000. One day when Sly was out, the bird and I really got into it and he put some serious holes in my hands and arms. When I couldn't take it anymore, I grabbed the bird by the neck, twisted it until it snapped and threw it on the ground.

When Sly came home he took one look and said, "What happened to the boid?"

I said, "I don't know, he was biting me and we got tangled up. We both twisted, and I accidentally tied a knot in his neck."

Sly wasn't happy. He said, "That boid was worth more than you."

I got very angry but held my cool. I said, "He ain't worth anything now."

Anyway, it was a great action fight and I won a unanimous decision. It is on YouTube today. McCall and I were both busted up, though, and I had to have twelve stitches in my eye. When I went by McCall's dressing room, I heard him screaming because of the needles they were using to patch him up. I walked in and grabbed his hand and held it tight until the stitching was over. Afterward, we both got teary-eyed and hugged. Like François had said after his fight with Henri, it was over—there was no reason to hold a grudge.

I next went to Richie and asked, "Where's my money?"

"Sly's got it."

"Well, I want to get paid, where is he?"

"I don't know."

I grabbed Richie by his throat and hit him with a left hook to his liver. Then I dragged him through the casino to the cage and several security officers swooped down on me. They had their batons ready. I said, "Yeah, you guys can overpower me, but not before I take one or two of you with me. "

One of them asked, "What's wrong, Mr. Curto? What's this all about?"

I said, "I give my heart and soul in that ring tonight and I didn't get paid."

The guards backed off. Richie arranged to get me $10,000 from the cage and I chalked up the rest of what I was owed as payment for Sly's bird. My relationship with Sly and Tiger Eye Productions was over.

* * *

My unemployment didn't last long. The cut in my eye had reopened during my tussle with Richie and I was walking around Caesars with David Gilmore (a huge Baby Huey-looking black trainer) dripping blood, when a heavyweight named Bernardo Machado approached us. He said with a stutter, "B-B-Bennie Curto, J-J-Joe Conforte wants to talk to you."

I said, "Who's he?"

David said, "Joe Conforte runs Mustang Ranch, the big whorehouse near Reno."

I'd heard of the place. It was a big time operation and had the reputation of counting entertainers and politicians among its clients.

Bernardo stuttered some more, but managed to get out that he had tickets to fly to Reno that night and that I should go with him. I was curious and since I had nothing else going, decided to take the trip.

I went to the ranch and met Joe and his wife Sally. She said to me with a country twang, "What you need Vinnie, is a manager. That there Hollywood star (Sly) is not a manager. I'm prepared to get you fights in Reno, Las Vegas, and all over the world."

I learned that with Sally money talked and bullshit walked. She opened up a suitcase that contained $200,000 cash and a four-year contract. I signed.

I had David Gilmore come to the ranch to train me, but after some six months I hadn't had a single fight. I ended up becoming a pimp and even serviced a female customer.

It started when a couple of the girls got fired and I talked to Sally for them and they got their jobs back. They were so appreciative they started giving me half of their earnings every week and called me "the Man."

And then one night I was in the kitchen chatting with a couple of the girls when the "floor maid" (who made sure all the customers were properly taken care of) came running in and said, "You've got to help Sally out right away. It's an emergency."

"What's wrong? Is Sally okay?"

"Yes, but a very important client came in with his wife and they both want to get serviced. We need someone to do his wife. Will you take care of her?"

I did what had to be done and the husband paid me $2,500 when I was through. I felt a little embarrassed about the whole thing, though. Later, when I was out driving around with David, I told him about it. He laughed and said, "Curto, you're a whore."

As we drove the car started swerving on occasion and I realized David must have had a few cocktails before we left the Ranch. I grabbed the wheel from him and pulled over to the side of the road, but it was too late. A black and white police cruiser pulled up behind us. Two redneck cops got out and for no reason, busted Gilmore's head open. When I made a move to help they pulled their guns and told me, "Shut up and don't move." They arrested David and gave me some kind of a bullshit ticket.

When I walked into the courthouse two weeks later those same two cops were in the lobby. I said, "If it isn't the tough guys with the batons and guns. If you take away the guns, I'll shove those batons up your asses." It was a dumb thing, but I couldn't help myself.

One of the cops shoved my head back real hard and I decked him with one punch. I downed the other one and then it seemed like the whole police force was on me. They threw me in the holding tank where David was awaiting his court appearance. He greeted me by saying, "Curto, welcome to the Graybar motel."

David was taken into the next room before the judge and got sentenced to ninety days. After the sentencing I heard the judge say, "Now, bring this guy who likes to hit police officers into my courtroom."

Hearing that, I just knew I was going to do at least a year. Before they took me out of the cell I said a prayer: *God, if I can get a break here I promise I'll go out and do something good with my life.*

God answered my prayers. The judge was the same guy who paid me to screw his wife at the Ranch. When he saw me he called the two cops to approach the bench. He said, "We're not doing this. The Mustang Ranch provides a valuable service in this community. Some guy with a grudge against cops and a gun says, 'I'm going to kill a cop today.' As he drives by the Ranch he decides to stop in and have some fun. When he leaves his anger is gone and a cop's life is saved. Case dismissed."

After that, I was pretty much through with Reno. It seemed like Sally and Joe would never get me a fight and I figured that they really wanted me there more for protection than anything else.

Sally really liked me, though, and before I left she started the ball rolling for me to fight Mark Frazie for the WBC Continental Americas light heavyweight title.

Chapter Seventeen

Chong-Pal Park and Another Brush with Death

After the Mustang Ranch I went back to Miami to see Angelo Dundee. He welcomed me with open arms and said, "I'm not your father, but I think of you as a son. You are bound to win a title."

The first fight Angelo got for me was against Zovek Barajas in Atlantic City, New Jersey, on March 22, 1983. I was so grateful I thanked Angelo and asked him, "Do you love me?"

He melted. "Well, Vinnie, when we get to heaven, where we *know* we are going, it will be all love, so we might as well get started right now. Yes, I love you."

I beat Barajas by technical knockout and got a couple more fights that I also won. Johnny Gio heard I was back on the east coast, so he set up a fight for me in Massachusetts against a guy named Clinton Longmire, who I beat on points on May 23, 1984.

Following that was the fight against Mark Frazie for the WBC Continental Americas light heavyweight title that Sally Conforte had opened the door for. I won on points. I had a fun little dialog with the audience afterwards, saying, "Everyone is saying how good I did with Frazie, but someone was kicking the shit out of me!" The crowd, which happened to include the main stars of MIAMI VICE, cracked up.

After the fight, Michael Mann and John Nicolella of the *Miami Vice* series asked me if I had ever done any acting. I laughed and said, "I've been kind of acting for years."

John said, "There is a young actor coming down from New York to star in the show; we'd like you to play his bodyguard. Are you interested?"

"Absolutely!"

When we started shooting the episode, the young actor's and my dressing room were in the same trailer. The actor's role was that of an abusive boyfriend, powerful and vicious. When I talked with him following the scene I said, "You were fantastic! I think you're going to go places."

I was right. The young actor was Bruce Willis.

Suddenly, I was rated the number one contender for Chong-Pal Park's IBF World Super Middleweight title. The fight was scheduled for June 30, 1985, at the Munhwa Gymnasium in Seoul, South Korea—Park's home turf. He was a heavy favorite and I knew I'd probably need to knock him out just to get a draw.

I also knew from Park's record that he could punch. He'd taken out some good fighters, including Murray Sutherland the previous July. Sutherland was a tough guy and he'd given the great Tommy Hearns all he could handle before losing a ten-round decision. Park definitely had my attention.

When I got into the ring that night and got a close look at Park, I was even more impressed. He had muscles everywhere including his eyeballs, and his arms were like telephone poles with sledgehammers at the end. Even today when I think of him I experience pain.

I fought a great fight, but after fifteen rounds I lost by unanimous decision. I believe that if we'd fought in Miami, *I* would have won by unanimous decision. But because judges in a fighter's hometown almost always are biased toward their hometown champion the decision went the other way.

My first world title shot was a bust.

***

After the Park fight, Johnny Gio got three more fights for me that I won; and then I hit a dry spell. I hung around Miami for months waiting for another bout, but nothing came through and I was running short of money.

I was in the gym one day when I spotted my old friend Charlie Migola. Charlie was really glad to see me again, but said he was disappointed over the bum rap I took over the Hagler thing. I told him that was in the past and I didn't think about it anymore. Then I said, "Things are pretty rough for me right now. Do you think your uncle Roberto would get behind me and open the door for some decent paying fights and maybe another title shot?"

Charlie said, "Maybe, but that will have to wait." He then leaned close and whispered, "We got a big shipment (of drugs) in but the boat ran aground. You can see it from the highway and nobody dares unload it. Nothing else is going to happen until we can get that taken care of."

I thought a few seconds and then said, "What if I unload it?"

Charlie stared at me and realized I was serious. "It's risky. You could end up in a lot of trouble."

"Right now I've got nothing in the works and not much to lose. I'm willing to take a chance."

Charlie took me to his uncle. I walked right up to Roberto and said, "Charlie told me about your problem. It would be an honor if you let me help you solve it."

A few hours later I was alone in a rowboat on my way to the drug boat, while Roberto and some of his men kept an eye on me from shore. As I rowed I saw a police car cruise by on the highway. I waved and kept on going.

Although it was night, a full moon provided all the light I needed, and the bales of coke were stashed exactly where Roberto told me they'd be. When I finally pulled into shore, the henchmen helped unload the rowboat and got the drugs out of there.

Roberto and his entire group were very appreciative, and I was pretty sure he'd use his clout to line something up for me. In the world of drug dealing nothing is ever certain, though, and something came up that took priority over my career. Some morons from another cartel bought product from Roberto, diluted it and tried to sell it back to him. An argument ensued and one of the scammers spit in Roberto's face. Roberto pulled out his gun and shot the guy, wounding but not killing him. It was the kind of thing that can lead to all-out war.

The next day I was on a plane with Charlie, Roberto, and some of his men, heading for South America and a sit down between Roberto and the other crew. I knew this could get pretty hairy and didn't really want to be there. However, Roberto wanted me along and told me he could get me a fight against Hagler, who had just won the middleweight title. That was too tempting an opportunity for me to ignore, so there I was.

About an hour before we landed, some of Roberto's men must have gotten nervous because they started passing around enough snow to shut down ten airports. *Great.*

When we got to the hacienda where the meeting was going to be held, Roberto and his lieutenants and the bosses of the other side sat down at a long table, facing each other. Things started going bad almost immediately with the leaders screaming at each other in Spanish. Even though we were badly outnumbered, Charlie got carried away and spit in the face of the top guy across from him. Within seconds Charlie's brain was splattered all over, including on my face.

There was no time to think—I just reacted. I remember the chaos going on around me as I dragged Roberto outside and toward the Jeep we were driving, dodging bullets on the way.

We were almost to the Jeep when I took part of a blast from a shotgun in my back just above the tailbone, and lost consciousness. I woke up in a hospital in Miami and my chart said I'd had a "cyst" removed. I don't know for sure what they actually did in the way of treatment, but the scar that remains today tells me they had to dig out a lot of lead. Roberto pulled some strings at the hospital and my injury wasn't classified as a gunshot wound. The cops weren't called and I was never questioned about what happened.

I was in the hospital for three weeks and when I got out, I stopped to see Roberto at his office. He was heartbroken over the loss of Charlie and I consoled him as best I could. He then told me he would continue to try to get me the Hagler fight.

I said, "Thanks, but after all that's happened my head isn't right. I'm not ready for Hagler. I need time before I get into the ring again."

He smiled sadly. "I understand and I'm very sorry."

As I headed for the door, he stopped me and handed me a small suitcase. "Here, take it. Don't say anything, just go."

I left. Later, when I opened the suitcase there was $187,000 cash in it.

Can you imagine what I could have done with that much money? Instead, in my depressed state I decided to end it all in one big blowout at the Dunes Hotel in Vegas. I bought an unmentionable amount of coke and a couple of girls to help ease my pain as I passed into the next world. But, as usual, it seemed like nothing could kill me. When I came out of my stupor a few days later, the girls and all my money were gone.

* * *

I'd passed on trying to get a fight with Hagler, but by some fluke I ended up as Ring Magazine's number one contender to fight Park again. I have no idea how they figured I deserved a second title shot, but they did, and I wasn't going to turn it down. The fight was set for April 11, 1986, at the Sports Arena in Los Angeles. A lot of my new Hollywood friends showed up and Bruce Willis sent me a cool telegram.

Although it had been several months since the fiasco with the drug dealers in South America and Charlie's death, I was still messed up in the head and not mentally ready for the fight. In spite of that I managed to stay even with Park and was even ahead on one score card going into the fifteenth round.

And then Park nailed me with a vicious punch, and I dropped like a sack of potatoes. As I hit the canvass, I heard my father's voice berating me—reminding me about the gun. I gave him my silent answer: *I'm going down and I'm taking you with me!*

Since then, I have learned not to blame *anyone else* for my life. It works out a lot better for me when I take responsibility for what I am and what I do. When it's all in my hands I can really do something about it.

* * *

I fell in love with movies at a young age. As a child I rarely saw movies, but the ones I did see had an enormous impression on me. When I was shining shoes, there was a theater that showed old hit movies running *Somebody up There Likes Me*, about the life of Rocky Graziano. One of the wise guys knew I wanted to be a boxer and some of what I was going through at home. He took me to that movie, and I couldn't get it out of my head. Through some rather odd events, I ended up living my dream in the acting business.

After the loss to Park, a friend thought he was doing me a favor and gave me some steroids. It was the only time I ever had tried them. It was horrible. He didn't really inform me how to use them, though. I am actually glad he didn't, because the fact that I couldn't use them probably saved my brain. So many fighters were seduced into using them with the promise of increased punching power. But the damage resulting from long-term use makes them more destructive than they are worth.

Just when I thought it couldn't get any worse, in early 1988 I got rear ended in a car accident and broke a bone in my neck. When I first got out of the car, I was really dizzy and attributed it to shock. The guy who hit me was mad and came over to hit me, but I hit him first. He sat down on the sidewalk and stayed put.

The cops came and asked what happened. I explained that I'd been rammed into from behind. I had no idea my neck was broken, so I didn't claim any injuries. It wasn't until I fought Al Houck in Minnesota in November 1988, that I realized how badly I was hurt. Houck hit me on the chin with a simple jab and my whole body went numb. I collapsed right there.

They rushed me to the hospital and found the broken bone in my neck. The doctors couldn't believe I had been able to function for so long with that serious an injury. I had to have a steel plate put in my neck and was told I should never fight again. *Yeah, right.*

As I was recuperating, a then powerful talent agent, Joe Kolkowitz, who was friends with other sports actors like O.J. Simpson, took me on. He sent me to a reading for a new series TV called *Amen*. It was a guest starring role, playing an emotionally troubled boxer who is embraced by the community. While I read, there was a guy up in bleachers in the dark, telling me how to play the role. He had me read my lines nine different ways. When I finished, I got the call back. The casting lady told me the guy was Ed Weinberger, who had produced *The Mary Tyler Moore Show* and *Taxi*.

The plot of the show had the church in *Amen* sponsoring me, but they decided to let a big pro manager take over my career. In the last scene of the show I got all emotional and started blubbering. And then the whole crew started crying. After that, Weinberger offered me a lead role for a series, but it didn't get picked up.

Through my role in *Amen* I landed appearances in *Quantum Leap, Walker, Texas Ranger,* and a part in a movie I will never forget, *Backstreet Dreams.* It starred Brooke Shields as a brilliant psychotherapist who diagnoses a troubled kid with autism and helps him and his father. I loved the role, and back then I loved Brooke. She was such a bright spirit, even with her mother hovering over her like a dragon with a pile of jewels. I knew the mother would not approve of me as a mate, so we remained just friends. Sometimes Brooke got dramatic on the set and made people think we were an item just to tease them. She will always be my friend. I also met Nick Cassavetes on the set, who later got me a role in another movie.

In May of 1991, I tried a fight in Reseda, California, just to see if I still had my chops. It ended as a "No contest."

Later in 1991, a friend called me and said there was a part just for me in a movie called *29th Street.* Set in a tough neighborhood in New York, it was about Frank Pesce's life. He was an actor who had appeared in several crime and boxing films—the kind of roles where he was always getting himself in trouble. It was right up my alley, and they hired me without even reading me! The storyline reminded me so much of my own life and Frank and I became fast friends. There is a funny excerpt from it on the front page of my website you will love, typical wise guy BS. It starred Anthony LaPaglia, Danny Aiello, and Lanie Kazan, great group.

I also met my long-time friend, actor and great stunt guy, Pete Antico, who has Tourette's syndrome except when he gets in front of a camera. We used to say if we could figure that out, we could cure the disease.

I loved performing so much that I began to look around for more ways to reach out to an audience.

Chapter Eighteen

Comic Relief

I had been doing a little standup routine fifteen minutes before some of my fights and getting an amazing reaction from the crowd. I would go into the ring nervous and tight, and by the time I finished my comedy routine both the audience and I were relaxed and happy. So, after the Park fight, I started going to the Comedy Store in West Hollywood for relief. One time on Open Mic Night I got up and hit it out of the park.

I told the audience about my fight with Park, "His name was Chong Pal Park and just saying his name causes me pain. He was about five feet ten when the fight started. Then there was this flash and when I looked at him again, he suddenly looked nine feet tall. Then I realized it was because I was on my ass looking up at him. There was a guy with a white shirt and black tie yelling numbers in my face. I stared at him, not comprehending what was going on. When he reached ten he waved his arms. That's when I realized it was all over and I'd been knocked out."

I had made up a rap about my life as a boxer and hit the audience with it:
They call me MC Vinnie
I'm a real cool guinea
I'm an ex pro fighter
Tryin' to make my future brighter.

If you don't think my act can entertain you
Better watch out sucker, or else I'll brain you.
Fifteen years, and ninety-four chances
Some were bangers, and some were dancers
Now I know I was never anybody's idol
Even though I fought for three world titles.
So, I moved onto something new and attracting
I went to Miami and started movie acting
Luck was with me when I rolled the dice
I ended up starring on a show called Vice
I met two guys named Johnson and Thomas
From that day on, I made myself a promise
To be bold with people and use a lot of honey
If you don't get the goal, you'll make a lot of money.
I left Miami with a champagne toast
And ended up living out on the West Coast.
Then one day I was down and depressed
Wanted to relax and get some rest
I came upon the Comedy Store
Owned by this bitch named Mitzi Shore.
Here I am not a pro as of yet
Everyone knows you are only as good as your last set
The object is to be paid regular
That doesn't mean knocking out some heckler
I finally found my remedy – this thing that we call Comedy.

The audience cracked up. After that I started hanging out with the top comics of the day and carried the props for Jim Carrey.

I got a break of sorts when Andrew Dice Clay got into a beef with another comic named Sam Kinison. Sam's guys were going to beat up Dice—they even pulled guns. I said, "I've been shot before by a shotgun. The guys that shot me were a hell of a lot badder than you. I stayed awake and fully able to function for forty-five minutes before I passed out from blood loss. If you don't hit a bullseye with your first shot, I'll do a lot of permanent damage before I go down."

They thought about it and backed off.

I acted as one of Dice's body guards and was always at his shows. One of the things that kept me busy was his habit of insulting girls in the audience. Sometimes their dates didn't think Dice was funny and wanted to wreak havoc on him after the show. Whenever Dice felt he was in trouble, he'd tell his then wife, Kathy "Trini" Swanson, "Trini, call Vinnie."

About this time, I began feeling lonely. I had almost always had a woman in my life, and usually there were one or two more who had a reservation pending. They would tell me, "If you ever finish with the one you're with, I'll be waiting for your call."

I started out with a girl named Jennifer, just to protect her. You would never know it by looking at her, but she was a whore. She and her pimp used to come to the Comedy Store to run into potential customers. But he was really mean to her—he even beat her up several times. The last time was after she was with me (for no money) for a week. I finally dropped him on his ass, and told him, "Any way you want to go; I know you have guns, knives, whatever. I'll give you a knife to fight me." Finally, he gave in and cut her loose. She and I went to Vegas and got married. For my birthday, she brought in a few friends, a very nice surprise.

When we broke up, it was because we really were more friends than anything. She was a better person than a couple of my so-called "normal" wives.

*　*　*

It was there I met a comedian named Mark Goldstein, a Yale graduate who was also a screenplay writer. He taught me how to write a screenplay—structure, character development, when and where to put plot points and a lot more. When he saw some of my practice writings he was impressed by my nearly flawless dialog. Thanks to his teachings, a new door opened for me.

I got an idea for a screenplay I called *Comedy Can Kill* (about a cop going undercover as a comedian), I asked Dice, who was working on *The Adventures of Ford Fairlane* along with Mark, to set me up with a meeting with Joel Silver to discuss the project. Dice didn't know I had met Joel Silver previously, and even trained him for a brief time.

Dice got back to me and said the meeting was on. The only trouble was Joel Silver wasn't there. Instead, another producer named Barry Josephson was there posing as Silver. As soon as I saw the scam I knew I had to get out before something bad happened.

That night I was at the Store and I said to Dice, "You had Barry Josephson posing as Silver? I *know* Silver. I *trained* him. What the fuck were you thinking?"

Dice shrugged. "What's this meeting thing all about? If you need money I can't help you right now. I didn't make much on my last tour."

I was pissed. "What did they pay you in, bricks? Here's another fucking brick for you." I slapped him hard across his face with my open hand. His eyes rolled in his head.

His other bodyguard was supposed to be a karate guy and a smirk spread across Dice's face when he saw the guy charge at me. When he got to me I hit him with a right hand and a left hook and he went down for the count. People came from all over and jumped on us—the whole pile went down.

While we were thrashing around on the floor, Dice grabbed my hair like a little girl. I got to my feet, pulled him up and smacked him again. This time he took off running down Sunset Boulevard. All the women in the front of the store started clapping and cheering me.

Years later the Comedy Store awarded me a crystal goblet with the words "I bitch slapped Dice Clay" engraved on it.

* * *

I got to know several of the other comedians very well, too. Sam Kinison was a great guy and I was saddened when I found out he died in a car accident on April 10, 1992. The other vehicle crossed lanes and ran into his car head on. Initially his injuries didn't look that serious, but minutes later he was dead. He was a very mystical and connected preacher before he got into comedy though, and before he left, his friend who was with him said he had a conversation with God. He said, "I'm not ready to go yet." He waited a beat, then apparently got his answer. He said, "OK, I will come now if you say it is time," and died.

Robin Williams was somebody else I got close to. He had also been abused as a child and he had great empathy for me.

One of my favorite people to hang out with was Rodney Dangerfield. Rodney was able to intake more coke than even my old contacts. We would go out and party with groups of people and occasionally we'd all wake up on the floor. I remember the time Rodney and I woke up at the same time. We looked at each other over the bodies piled up on the floor and he said, "Things are rough! Judging by this particular situation, I'd have to say I truly killed about three hundred audience members."

Another great comedian there was Joe Rogan, funny guy but very tough too. He didn't let any idiot in the audience bother him, and usually just rolled off any heckling with an even better joke. He and I got into a small beef once (over something stupid I'm sure), and we almost came to blows, but he didn't back down, then we made friends. I have the highest respect for Joe Rogan; I can honestly say he is a 100% real, decent human being.

* * *

Anyway, with the help of Mark Goldstein (who passed away in 2008) I wrote the entire script for *Comedy Can Kill*.

After that I wrote a treatment about my life titled *Out on My Feet*. I was out knocking on doors giving out the treatment and stopped at a place called Propaganda Films. This nasty woman at the reception desk didn't want any part of me. She ordered me out, screaming and threatening.

I said, "If you read my story you will know you are not going to scare me."

One of the directors, Greg Gold, stepped into the office and the woman stopped screaming. I explained to him why I was there and handed him the treatment. He took a brief look and said he didn't like the format. He added that my method of getting noticed would not get me the kind of attention I was looking for.

I admitted he was probably right, and then asked him to please read the treatment. I told him it was the kind of story that could help save the lives of some kids. He said to leave it with him, and he'd get back to me. When I walked out I wasn't sure if he'd really read it or had just wanted to get rid of me.

A month went by before Greg called me. He said, "Vinnie, you have to go to a meeting at the Café Roma. There are some people who read *Out on My Feet* and really liked it, and one of them is a big name."

I wasn't very optimistic but went to the meeting anyway. I met Barry Primus (an actor in *Cagney and Lacey*), and some bearded guy in a wool cap I didn't know. Barry explained the "big name" was none other than Robert De Niro. He had read the script and really liked it. With a trace of sarcasm, I said, "Yeah, I'm sure he does."

The guy in the wool cap said, "It's true, I do like it." It was De Niro. I hadn't recognized him in the cap and beard.

We made a deal for me to work with writer Larry Golin, the brother of Propaganda Films co-founder Steve Golin, on the *Out on My Feet* project. We were off to the races.

Little did I know what a wild ride the future held for me.

***

Through my time in the film and TV business, I met some of my favorite people. At Propaganda Films, I ran into Sean and Chris Penn (God rest his soul). Sean was interested at one point in doing the story about my little friend François, and I got to know his brother Chris really well. Chris lived right on Ocean Avenue in Santa Monica, and we used to pal around together and make everyone around us laugh. But there was a deep sadness about him. That combination of cheerful comic and deep feelings made him a tremendous actor. You can see it in a little part he had in *Rush Hour*. It was comedic, but you saw so many layers inside him at the same time.

One time I asked Chris to take a walk with me. I told him whenever he was ready, I wanted him to trust me and open up to me. He said, "I know you are a full human being and you don't have any mental problems."

I said, "What are you, a wise ass?"

He answered, "Yes!" One of his favorite sayings was, "Seagulls and mermaids understand me."

Even though he had issues, he was a phenomenal human being. When I had a beef with my friend Pete Antico and his wise guy friends back east, I was really sweating because I had to go back and resolve the problem before it got even bigger. It was right before Christmas, I had no money at all, and it was $1,000 for a coach seat on an airplane.

Chris came to my rescue. He told his manager to get me business class seats at $2,500. The manager protested, but Chris knew how important it was to me and forced the guy to buy not only the ticket but a new suit for me as well.

When I got to the sit down, Pete had his guy with him. He looked me up and down, somewhat respectfully, I thought, but I knew the decision was still in doubt. Then my guy pulled up and Pete's buddy turned sycophant. My man was way senior to Pete's friend in the Mob hierarchy and

Pete's guy became very polite and submissive. But Pete was doing his Tourette's thing, pointing his finger and mouthing expletives. I quickly intervened, explained Pete's condition, and that he didn't mean any disrespect. Everybody ended up making friends and the situation was resolved. When Pete and I got back to California we went out together for dinner in Malibu and everything was fine.

Chris and I had the time of our lives acting together on the movie *Stealing Harvard*, a hysterical story about a totally straight guy who turns to crime to help his niece pay for her tuition at Harvard.

After a long day of shooting on the movie (we played characters who hung out together), we went to a bar for a couple of beers. One of guys at the bar started saying bad things about Sean, loudly. Chris asked, "Can you guys keep it down?"

They responded, "Oh, you are the big movie actor, so we all have to do what you say? You'd better watch your step."

Chris really wanted to teach them a lesson for the nasty comments about his brother, but we were outnumbered so he called a couple of friends to come help. They never showed and the bad boys kept making derogatory comments like, "Look at the pussy actors; everything is fake about them."

I warned them, "Yeah, he's an actor, but he can punch like Joe Louis, and I was a fighter for 26 years. But let's not fight, let me buy you a beer."

One of the guys tried to sucker punch me but Chris threw a round house right hand. He was so strong and knew how to use all his weight to back it up. I was astonished, but we made short work of them. It was something Chris never forgot. Unfortunately, Chris never resolved his problem. He died on January 24, 2006, at the age of forty, of a cardiomyopathy condition—which some scientists now say can come from a broken heart.

I have this recurring dream: a lot of my friends and relative who have passed away sit down with me at this huge table.

We laugh and eat, but at the end of the night, they shoo me away. I see Chris there sometimes and some of the people from my childhood, it's so real. Sometimes I feel Chris around me and then I see him in a movie or something; it's really eerie but comforting all at the same time.

I saw my mother there one time and she looked so young and beautiful, plus she told me she loved me. I knew I was dreaming, because she never told me that in my life. She told me things were very different where she was. I got the feeling that she was trying to tell me all the reasons she was jealous of me were gone.

My heart nearly broke at Chris's funeral when they lowered his casket into the grave. I was blubbering and almost jumped in the hole after him. A pair of strong arms saw my intention and grabbed me gently, but firmly. The man told me if I ever needed a friend to call him and gave me his phone number. It was Jack Nicholson—my final gift from Chris.

I called Jack a few times after that and had great conversations with him. He is another unique gem of a human being.

When I got cast in a movie with Pamela Anderson, *Barbed Wire*, I met another great guy who became one of my closest friends, David Hogan, the director who had won more awards for music videos than anyone on the planet. He was a very cool guy and invited me to live at his hacienda on the beach in Malibu. David would later be one of the keys to opening up my film life at a much higher level.

* * *

I had stopped doing business with my associates back east, but something about me acting in these gangster-related movies got the feds all worked up about me. One morning I looked out the window and saw a car with a guy in it watching me. I got into my car and almost eluded him, but then another car came around in front of me and I was blocked. They were investigators and said they wanted to talk with me. They brought me in to an office and started showing me pictures. They said, "We just want to know a couple things about a few of the people you know."

Then they asked me if I knew this one big guy. I said, "Never heard of him." Big mistake. They had a picture of me and the guy laughing and me slapping him on the back. "Oh, that's right, I met him at a party," I said.

They said if I gave them some information, they would help me out if I ever got in trouble. They kept grilling me about a lot of details of my life. I told them how many fights I'd had and that I suffered from really serious memory loss.

They put me in handcuffs and flew me to Seattle, where I had hidden out for a while during the Hagler thing. Then we went to a couple more cities where I had some history. They were really mad because they couldn't get anything out of me. They finally dropped me off at the Dallas airport with no shoes or socks.

I called Gio who, along with about twenty other guys in New England, had been really worried, and he got me a ticket home.

A couple years later, they chased me down again and subpoenaed me to the grand jury in New York, where Rudy Giuliani was the US Attorney. Indictments were handed down and a trial followed. It was revealed during the trial that any time Vito Antuofermo fought in Vegas, if he was still standing at the end, he would get the decision.

I yelled out in the court room, "I knew I beat you Vito!"

Everyone cracked up, including Vito. He laughed and said he would give me a rematch.

I had an amazing attorney named Sherman Edelberg. When I testified, Giuliani was ripping into me and was getting uncomfortably close on a couple of issues I didn't want to talk about. Sherman objected. He said, "Mr. Giuliani, seems to know more about this case than anybody, and his questions are way out of bounds. Therefore, I plan to call him as a witness."

Giuliani was removed as the lead prosecutor and the heat was off.

Chapter Nineteen

The Fight Is On

In 1993, I was still doing comedy and also working as a bouncer. I was married to the sister of another girl I had previously dated for several years. The girl I had dated was Sophie Goros, a beautiful but powerful, almost overwhelming, and headstrong Greek. Her favorite statement was, "Here's what we do! Here's what we do!" She was so tough she could have fought with guys in the street. She had a great punch with a lot of power. But after a while, it was a bit much.

I had always admired her younger sister, Olga, and must have really liked the Greek strain, because I had a brief fling with their mother as well. Anyway, Olga and I hit it off and we settled down in Sherman Oaks, California, with our two kids, Michael and Loretta.

I started working as a bouncer at nightclubs because it was good pay and I was actually better at settling fights by negotiation than by using my fists, which the bar owners loved. Whenever a gang came in, I would make friends with all of them. If a problem broke out, I would summon them all to my side and the problem disappeared. The club owners were so impressed they asked if any of my "friends" would like jobs. The amazing thing was, they *did* want to work, and many of them dropped out of the gangs and settled down.

A year went by uneventfully, until one afternoon as I was waiting at a traffic light in Van Nuys, when I saw a big black guy berating a couple of teens in the street. The light turned green, but the black man continued yelling at the kids. Impatiently, I beeped the horn. "Hey pal, move your big ass," I said. I laid on the horn again and moved forward, forcing the guy and the teens to cross the street, then I continued driving down Van Nuys Boulevard.

Next thing I knew, a white van pulled up beside me. I turned to look, and it was the guy who had been in the altercation with the kids. He lowered his window and I did the same. He hollered to me, "You got a big mouth."

I said, "That would be correct. I can back it up, too."

The guy motioned to an empty parking lot. I pulled in and jumped out of my car. He met me in the middle of the lot and fired off a left-right combination, nailing me square on the chin. My knees buckled a little, but I shook it off. I said out loud, "My chin is still good." That seemed to confuse him. He then said, "Don't sing it, bring it!"

This brother could fight his ass off. He had a picture-perfect left jab and a "smart bomb" right hand. He really knew what he was doing. His left jab had my head popping back and forth. He smiled, "This here's a left jab, baby."

I said, "Don't 'baby' me. Because in about five minutes you're going to be calling me your "daddy," son.

He said, "Yeah, white boy? Keep running your mouth."

I fired off four body shots. A long visceral groan emerged from his mouth.

Suddenly, a black and white police car pulled up. An officer rolled down his window, smiling, and asked what was going on. The black man bent forward, taking a couple of deep breaths, and said, "I'm teaching this punk how to fight. Under his breath he added, "Or he's teaching me."

The two cops smiled, saying, "Carry on," and drove off. As soon as they were gone, I hit him with two more body shots. The guy doubled over with another long groan. I felt bad for him, and told him, "Just tell me you quit. Just tell me you quit." I said. "It's not about black and white, it's about man to man."

He moaned again and shook his head "no."

I feigned a shot to the head and drove a straight right hand to his body. The strain on his face said it all. I fired off two more "seal the deal" body shots that were strategically placed just under his heart, close to the solar-plexus.

The guy finally gave in. "Okay! I've got to quit. I'm a cop. Those sweet young kids you seen me screaming at are my prisoners. If I were to let you walk all over me, what do you think they would have done?"

When those two cops didn't do anything, I should have known. I walked over to him with my hand out to shake, but he didn't immediately accept my gesture. I stopped and just looked at him for a few seconds and then he dropped his offensive posture. He said, "Sorry man, it's over." We hugged. I laughed and told him at least we had a good work out. He looked at my face and laughed at how swollen it was.

When I got back to my apartment, the kids looked at my enlarged face in horror. Olga started screaming. She thought I had been in an accident. She asked me what happened, and I told her I had been in a fight. She said, "Aren't you glad you aren't fighting anymore?" I smiled and I told her that today I had gotten one more shot at boxing. Olga and the kids, almost in unison, said I looked like I had a lot more than *one* shot.

I went looking for my gym bag, singing, *Ain't No Stopping Me Now*. I found it, laughed, and picked up the phone to call Chuck Talhami, my old trainer. I shocked him by telling him I wanted to make a comeback. He asked me how I would make a comeback, and I told him that José Sulaiman of the WBC had told his son who was helping him run it before he passed (that actually didn't happen until 2014) that if I ever wanted to make a comeback, he'd help me secure a title shot. He knew I had been robbed with the Hagler thing and wanted to make it right.

Then Chuck shocked me. He said Anthony, my then nineteen-year-old son from a relationship I'd had in Miami in 1974, was fighting in Miami. The local sports writers were comparing him to me. He quoted from a newspaper article, "Although he's a giant compared to his father, the resemblance is unmistakable, an uncanny defense, almost impossible to hit with a handful of rice."

Chuck said Anthony had won the Golden Gloves, and had a fight coming up the next week.

I flew to Miami and went to the Fifth Street Gym. What memories I had as I bounced up the front stairs and went inside. A tall, good-looking white kid and an equally good-looking, but short, black kid were sparring. As I walked up, the fighters stopped, got out of the ring, and took off their headgear and gloves. I told the tall guy that he had a pretty good jab, which is the most important punch in the business. He smiled and said, "My father used to say that."

I introduced myself and out of the blue, he landed that left jab on my chin. I told him he had better have a good reason for hitting me or I would respond with a lot worse.

It turned out the young man who slugged me was Anthony. I hadn't seen him since he was an infant and we hadn't recognized each other. He obviously was not happy with me.

I asked him about his mother, Charlene. I told him I had loved her very much, but she had a severe drug problem and would disappear for days at a time. She would come back covered with bruises and never explained how she got them. It was bad enough she was running with Cuban drug dealers, and they didn't want me to straighten her out. They sent me a message to back off or be killed.

I said I just couldn't deal with her issues and the insanity that was going on in my own life and career at the time, so we split. I let him know I returned and begged Charlene to give up the drugs, and then we could get back together and have a normal life. She wouldn't, though. That was the last time I had seen her or him.

Anthony told me I would never see Charlene again—she had passed away recently. He said she always spoke of me with love and respect. She told him I was a great man and kept all my fight clippings in a scrap book. I asked him for a chance to prove my love for him and his mother, but he shook his head and walked away. I couldn't think of anything I could possibly say that could make things right.

The next day José Sulaiman's son told me he would give me a chance to fight for the title in the new Super Cruiserweight class. All I had to do was win five fights sequentially.

I didn't envy my opponents. I was a man on a mission and nothing or nobody was going to stand in my way.

* * *

At the same time that I was doing standup and hanging out at Propaganda Films, I was still training at a local gym called Brothers Boxing Gym in Winnetka, California. The owner was Jim Moriarty, a kind, light-hearted soul. He owned the house and had a large garage that he had turned into a big gym that all the local kids visited. Jimbo, as we called him, had a soft spot for me, and when I fought with my wife, he would let me sleep in the ring in the gym. I helped train some of the kids who wanted my help whenever I was around.

When I told Jimbo I got the title shot, he went nuts. It was like a reward for him for all the totally selfless work he had always done for no money and no recognition. His wife was a real heartless person, so the kids and boxing were the only loves he had in his life. When I decided to go for the title, Jimbo personally worked with me for many hours to fine-tune my performance, and even paid for sparring partners.

One thing very exhilarating about this gym was there was zero hot water. We all had to get used to freezing showers. *Ouch*. They would wake you right up. I did at one point get a fungus from no chlorine and no hot water on my back, so please, don't any of you who have a gym repeat this habit.

There was the funniest guy at his gym. He was a young Latino who trained us and tried to clean up after us. He loved to watch cartoons, especially Mighty Mouse. He would sit in front of the TV every single time the cartoon was on and laugh.

Between working and spending so much time at that gym and Propaganda Films, Olga got fed up and took the kids and moved back to Boston to be with her family.

I also trained with another energetic Latino guy named Felix who had a hot Cuban girlfriend, Emma. When she and I first set eyes on each other there was instant chemistry. She was super intelligent and could speak about anything going on in the world. But it never went anywhere between us because I was only interested in one thing at the time, the world title.

Chapter Twenty

The Countdown Begins

On November 12, 1994, the first of my five fights was held in Greensburg, Indiana. My opponent was Tyrone Bledsoe.

As I walked up to the arena, I saw a young boy and his father waiting outside with an old decrepit movie camera. The boy said his father— a very humble and beaten down looking man—was a big fight fan and asked me if I would stand with his father while he took a little footage. After shooting for a few minutes, the father apologized for bothering me. I said, "It's fine. I was glad to do it. I'll see you inside."

The father said they couldn't afford tickets, but they had seen my picture and read about me in the paper and knew what I had been through. They knew my whole boxing history and wanted to meet me and wish me well. I told him this fight was not for the title, but for sure they were coming in as my guests. The kid looked shocked and the father was all choked up. I took them in with me and sat them ringside.

Tyrone Bledsoe was a tall, young black man. He was undefeated with a record of eighteen wins and no losses, with three draws. In his corner was one of the all-time great junior welterweight boxing champions, Aaron Pryor. Pryor and I had sparred together many times in the Fifth Street Gym. I walked right up to them and fixed Tyrone with my most menacing glare. He said, "Yo, I ain't heard no bell."

I pointed at Pryor and said, "Maybe not for you, but we've heard plenty of bells between us."

Tyrone said, "Yea, baby, you're probably his (Pryor's) age, but it's me you facin' tonight."

I said, "Young man, I hope you're ready. You're gonna go to school tonight."

I then turned to Aaron and said, "It's really good to see you, man." We hugged each other and then I went to my corner, leaving Tyrone shaking his head.

When the fight finally started, I worked Tyrone over pretty good. The sweat flew off his face at the end of a round when I nailed him with two unanswered three-punch combinations. We both walked back to our corners, but Tyrone was wobbling a little.

Aaron had to work overtime in the corner, rubbing Tyrone's legs, pouring cold water on the back of his neck and between his legs.

When the final bell rang, we waited in our corners for the official decision. The referee took the paper slips from the judges and tallied them. Then he said, "We have a unanimous decision. All three judges score the fight, five rounds to one for the winner ... *Vinnie Curto.*"

I climbed out of the ring and rushed over to the boy and his father, hugging them both. I told them to wait a minute and ran over to Pryor to walk him back to meet the old man and his son. "Aaron Pryor, I want you to meet two fans of mine and giant fans of yours."

I then said, "Aaron, how many title defenses did you have?"

"Vinnie, a *lot*. I don't even remember the number."

I said, "Damn, I'm glad I don't have that problem. Now, what were we talking about?" Everybody laughed.

Aaron called Tyrone over to take some pictures. Then we all hugged, and I wished Tyrone good luck. When I got my purse, I took $100 and gave it to the kid and his father.

My next fight was ten days later on November 22, at the Adam's Mark Hotel in Indianapolis, against Alphonso O'Hara. He charged me at the opening bell. I side-stepped and tattooed him. A quick one-two at the beginning of the second round followed by a left hook, finished him off.

I didn't fight again until July 9, 1995, in Boise, Idaho. That third fight was a scheduled ten-rounder against Ernie Valentine. Through some very bizarre circumstances, I almost lost my chance at the promised title fight.

I was sparring in the gym preparing for Valentine and noticed this older kid beating the heck out of a younger and smaller kid. Unable to keep my mouth shut, I walked over to them and said to the older guy, "How would you like it if I smacked you around for a few rounds?"

He accepted my offer and I gave him a little of his own medicine. I noticed an older man watching us with great interest. When we finished our session, I found out the spectator was the guy's father. His last name was Wooten. I think his first name was Ted or Tom, but I can't remember for sure after all these years. It turned out he had a lot of clout locally, though. But the main thing I remember about him is his smile—which was actually a smirk. It was something that would come back to haunt me. Anyway, the elder Wooten wasn't happy about me showing his son up. *Too bad*, I thought, and forgot about it.

On fight night, my first two rounds against Valentine were tough. Then I started to come on strong. After the bell ended the sixth round, I went to my corner and sat down. Before the bell for round seven, the referee waved for me to get up and come to the center of the ring. *What the hell?*

Confused, I did as instructed. As I walked, I looked into the crowd and sitting in a ringside seat smirking at me, was papa Wooten. I knew I was in trouble as the referee announced, "This bout has been changed from ten rounds, to six. The winner by split decision is Ernie Valentine."

There were cheers and some boos from the crowd. I looked at Wooten again as the smile on his face seemed to widen.

In stunned silence, I left the ring and went to my dressing room. After I showered and changed, I walked slowly, head down, out of the building and into the parking lot. I knew this loss would probably cost me my title shot and my comeback would be over. *Unbelievable.*

When I looked up, I saw a couple of figures across the lot. When I got closer, I recognized the older man and his son I'd met in Greensburg. After the night I'd had, it was good to see their friendly faces. I asked them, "You guys come a long way. I apologize that you made the trip and had to see me lose."

The boy said, "Vinnie, my dad got his check, but we could only afford one ticket. He let me go inside to watch and he waited out here." He then held up a video recorder and continued, "I used the $100 you gave us to buy a better camera and I recorded your fight. If anybody thinks you lost, have them watch this tape."

I took the tape from him and then we all hugged. Maybe I wasn't dead in the water after all. I now had some evidence that I had been robbed and I wasn't going to go down easy.

I jumped into my car and drove nearly non-stop for over thirty hours to the French Quarter in New Orleans, where the World Boxing Council Convention was in progress at the Maison Dupuy Hotel.

In wrinkled clothes, with messed hair and needing a shave, I walked into the convention hall. Jose Sulaiman was making a speech and stopped abruptly at my entrance.

I greeted everyone, then said, "I traveled far and fast to get here to plead my case. I'm forty-one-years old and won the first two fights of my comeback. But last night I lost on a hometown split decision because two of the officials happened to be blind." Everybody roared in laughter. I was on a roll.

I continued, "I have several kids who are going to wonder what I did after my career ended on such a sour note. I want to be able to give them the truth, and in this case, I have the truth here in my hand." I raised the tape for everyone to see. "This is a recording of that fight—the one I supposedly lost. I don't want to be written off because of this one decision. I would like the officials here to view this tape. Afterward, I will abide by whatever decision they reach."

Jose Sulaiman walked over and hugged me. He took me over to some officials and they all reconvened to an office to view the fight tape. At the conclusion, Sulaiman was furious and barred Boise from ever hosting a WBF or WBC fight.

Another of the officials said, "It's very clear that you won this fight. But it was against a fighter that was not in your category. One of the contenders for the WBC Cruiserweight Championship is present here and we want to see you box with him tomorrow in the gym. If you still have the legs, the chin, and the stamina, we'll continue the promise we made for your right to fight for the title."

I left the meeting feeling very upbeat. I would get one more chance to prove myself. I got into my car and drove around until I found a cozy spot to park. Grabbing my blanket and pillow and snuggled down in the back seat and went to sleep.

The next day, all the officials were sitting at ringside. Within earshot, some guy said to my opponent "Put a hurtin' on this guy. Take him out of his misery."

The fighter said, "Don't worry, you know I will be kickin' his ass. What's he, old enough to be my grandfather?"

When the bell sounded, the cocky bastard charged across the ring and threw a wicked left and right that caught nothing but air. I countered, tagging him with a solid three-punch combination.

When the bell rang again, my opponent let both hands fly, throwing bombs that landed nowhere. I took it to him, pummeling him in his own corner. When the bell rang to end the session, I ripped my headgear off.

I said to the assembled officials, "Is there any question about my ability to perform? Is there any question about my ability to compete? Please give me my last chance; I'll make you proud."

My adversary chimed in, "What the hell you people lookin' at? I'm glad I boxed his ass. Maybe we'll get together for real in the future, who knows? Now, give him his damn license!"

My comeback was back on track.

Chapter Twenty-One

The Final Test

I had two more tune-up fights to get through before my shot at the big prize of the Super Cruiser Weight world championship. Both were held at the Lady Luck Casino in Davenport, Iowa. On May 16, 1996, I beat Torman Doaks by TKO. On July 14 I got another TKO win over Lamont Ware. I was ready for my chance.

Shortly after the Ware fight, I signed to meet Jimmy Haynes in the title fight. It would be in Lincoln, Nebraska, on September 20, 1996, under the World Boxing Federation banner.

Haynes was born in Kentucky on Christmas day in 1965, ten years after I came along. That was one thing in his favor. He was big—over six feet—and known as being very tough and a hard puncher. I knew that between his age advantage and skills, he'd be a dangerous opponent. But that was okay. I never expected to win a championship in a cake walk.

It turned out Haynes was a good guy, though, and we treated each other with respect before and during our fight. The year following our match, he fought future heavyweight champ Vitali Klitschko and lost in four rounds.

* * *

As I pulled into downtown Lincoln, I was impressed with how quaint it was. It gave me the distinct impression of a small, friendly city.

I entered the hotel with bags in hand and spotted coffee and pastries in the lobby. I walked over to the table, dropped some pastries into my garment bag, then approached the front desk to check in. I was signing in when something caught my eye. It was a fight poster advertising the title fight. When I finished at the desk I walked up to the poster and stared at it for a several seconds before going to my room. That poster made it all real. It wasn't a dream any longer. I was going to fight for a world championship.

I unpacked and lay down on the bed, staring at the ceiling. I was content and felt a smile cross my face. I fell asleep thinking of my father. I dreamed I was watching my father pace back and forth in front of me again, then producing a gun and placing it on the kitchen table. I ran into my room. He said, "Asshole! Get in here *now*."

Reluctantly, I walked into the kitchen, saying, "Yeah, Dad"

He said, "Come here! Remember, if you don't become champ of the world, you've got to take a gun and put it to your head."

In the dream, I was suddenly all grown up. I walked straight up to my father and said, "It's over, Pops—it's all over. You're dead. I'm still alive and intend to live a long life."

Raising my voice, I yelled at him, "I will never be like you. I love my kids and will *never* do to them what you did to me."

He swung at me, but I blocked the punch and delivered a solid one of my own. In the next scene, two ambulance guys were carrying him out on a stretcher. He beckoned to me to come close and said, "I did you wrong, Vinnie"

I answered, "That's right, Dad. I'm not gonna repeat what you did to me on any of my kids and *you'll* never touch them either."

He finally smiled and said, "That's it, Champ. Now you're talking. I gotta go. I love–"

Just before he could complete telling me he loved me, the phone rang, waking me up. It was Chuck Talhami. He said, "Come get me you bastard. I'm at the airport."

I thought he was teasing me, making up for all the times I had teased him. Then he said, "I started with you, Vinnie, and I'll finish with you."

I got emotional and started crying so hard Chuck had trouble understanding me. I finally got out, "Don't move. I'll be right there."

With Chuck at my side, I trained with a dedication I hadn't felt in a long time. My son Anthony even surprised me by showing up in town to attend the fight and cheer me on.

* * *

Finally, September 20 arrived. Now was the time. Lincoln was the place. And I was the man.

Chuck and I smiled at each other as we stood in the middle of the ring and listened to the referee's instructions. When he finished, Haynes and I touched gloves and went back to our corners.

When the bell rang, I immediately established my left jab. I believe I won the round on the jab alone. The second round was a repeat of the first, with my left jab scoring at will. I was off to a good start, but that came to an end in the third.

When the bell sounded for that round, Haynes unleashed a vicious left hook that caught me flush and left me almost helpless against the ropes. Haynes pummeled me and my mouthpiece went flying out and landed in the ringside seats.

The referee was watching closely and I'm sure he was on the verge of stopping the bout. *Not tonight.*

Suddenly, I heard a voice, "Get *off* the damn ropes. Get *off* the damn ropes."

It sounded like my father was resurrected and was in the stands somewhere. Boy did I listen.

I tied Haynes up in a clinch and moved him toward the center of the ring. I knew I had to throw some punches to show the referee I was okay and to not end it. The only problem was, which opponent should I throw punches at? There were still three of them in front of me. But the cobwebs cleared quickly, and I had weathered the storm.

In the fourth round I started really turning it on. My forty-one-year-old legs and torso were performing magnificently. Haynes may have been ten years my junior, but you never would have known it. Rounds five thru eleven were repeats.

I was getting very hot and between each round Chuck and my cut man (a Cuban guy I didn't know) worked feverishly to cool me off. They put ice on the back of my neck, ice water down my pants, and Vaseline all over my face.

After the eleventh, Chuck said, "Three minutes, Vinnie. Three minutes, and you're champ of the world."

I told him, "Chuck, I want these last three minutes to be the best. Watch me this round."

I was sure I was ahead on all the score cards but didn't want to leave anything to chance—like in Boise. So, I went out for that final round like a demon. I attacked Haynes's body with ferocity, and his head with precision. The crowd was going berserk as my onslaught continued—cheering wildly with every punch I landed. I looked out at the ringsiders and saw a familiar face. It was my old nemesis, Mr. Wooten. He wasn't smirking now. The expression on his face was one of pain. Now it was my turn to smile. I grinned at him and fought even harder.

I heard Chuck holler, "No, Vinnie, stay away and box. Just jab and stay away."

To hell with that.

In desperation, Haynes threw another vicious left hook that landed. I didn't buckle and instead I returned one of my own. It caused Haynes to go wobbly and again the crowd went nuts.

Those last three minutes of my boxing career were fabulous. I displayed class and almost flawless execution. I n those 180 seconds of my final bout, I brought my craft to the highest level. I don't think many fighters of my age could have done any better. I couldn't think of a better way to say goodbye to something that was a part of me for so long.

Just before the final bell rang, I landed a jab and a right hand, with a left hook behind it.

Time seemed to stand still as the announcer looked at the score cards and summoned Haynes and me to center-ring. And then he said, "The winner by unanimous decision and the new Super Cruiserweight Champion of the World, is Vinnie Curto." I was euphoric and tears of joy and relief flowed freely.

I called Jim Moriarty at Brothers Boxing Gym soon afterward. He said, "Vinnie, give me the good news."

I said, "Jimbo, I'm the new champion."

There was dead silence, followed by sniffling sounds. Then, "Come back, c'mon, we've got to celebrate."

It was such a joy to share the excitement with him—a reward for all his selfless work for the kids, and me in particular. Jimbo passed away on April 21, 2008.

* * *

Later that night in my hotel room, with my championship belt still wrapped around my waist, I talked with Anthony. I thanked him over and over for coming to Lincoln to be with me. I told him, "I'm not too good at thanking anybody. If you knew my whole life, you'd understand that. But I want to just give you a little advice. Whatever you do in life, make sure you really want to do it. Have a passion for it. As you know, empty cans make the most noise. So, walk calmly in your path, but embrace life every day like it's your last."

I loosened the belt, walked over to Anthony and wrapped it around his waist. As I did, I said, "It fits you better than it will ever fit me. I know your mother is in heaven smiling down on us."

We embraced and I reached up and grabbed his head, pulling it forward and kissing his face a hundred times. I said, "Whatever you do, when you leave know that no matter what part of the world you are in or what your situation is, I love you."

He replied, "And I love you too, Dad."

For the second time that night, tears of joy flowed as Anthony walked out of the room.

EPILOGUE

After I won the title, the enthusiasm for *Out on My Feet* seemed to skyrocket.

A lot of the top actors of the day auditioned for parts. James Franco and Mark Wahlberg competed to play me. It was close, but Mark won. He had just finished *Boogie Nights* and was very hot.

Another plus was that Mark was also from one of the Boston hoods and we got along well, swapping crazy stories about Whitey Bulger and Joe Barboza. We laughed about the time Joe Barboza was running from some wise guy hitmen down our street (Chelsea Street) and you could hear all the gunshots.

I told him about the time my mother was sitting on the couch and my sister was sitting to the right of her. I was on the floor in front of her and my brother was on the side. A bullet came through the wall and hit a spring inside the couch. If not for that spring, it would have killed my mother and maybe me.

Later, when my mother and I were coming out of Tiny's Grocery Store, two guys approached us and said, "Lady, that bullet wasn't meant for you." My mother nearly wet her pants.

Tiny was a big six-foot-three tub of shit, but did have a soft spot in his heart. My mother would sometimes go into his store to steal food and he would always catch her, but let it go. Years later he told her, "How could I take food out of your kids' mouths?"

Mark and I were having a great time hitting the nightclubs until we ran into Leonardo DiCaprio. I tried to speak with him, and he just nudged me out of the way. I was very patient with him and his rejection, until he elbowed me really hard and gave me his back. I turned him around and hit him with a left hook to the body. Mark told me to get the hell out of there.

The thing that hurt the most was I was a big fan of Leonardo's and was very disappointed. If that had happened today, though, I would have bowed down to him, as he has become one of the major investors in a world-changing company called Beyond Meat. Beyond Meat makes vegetarian hamburgers that to me taste and cook exactly like regular hamburgers. They are made with pea protein instead of soy or gluten and are super healthy. I eat at least one a week.

One day when I came to the shoot, the teamster guys and production staff were tearing down the sets. *What the fuck?*

They were really mad that they hadn't been paid. One of the teamsters swung on me and landed. But then he ran into my left hook. If I catch you with that punch and you don't go down, you will do some funny things while standing up. This guy went down. I helped him up and told him, "I got hurt worse than you."

Holding his battered mouth, he said, "No you didn't." We made up and everything was okay. Then I found out what everybody was pissed off about and why the sets were being taken down.

It turned out the money-guy who had agreed to arrange the financing for the film, was not as solid as he first seemed to be. He never actually did the paperwork necessary to have the right to do the movie at all. So, when his money source fell through, he was not able to get another financial backer, despite the amazing cast we had.

People became paranoid after that. They were afraid that the script had some legal strings attached (which we found out from the bankruptcy court recently is not true) and didn't want to get involved.

Since then, I have thought a lot about why the movie fell apart. I feel part of the reason it didn't happen was that most of us involved (other than Barry, Larry, and the De Niro/Wahlberg crew) were running around in a sort of selfish excitement, boasting about what was about to happen. You know what Shakespeare said about pride: It goeth before a fall.

None of the people who I had helped when they truly needed it showed up for me at this time. I think now I wasn't in the right state of mind to utilize the movie to do what I was really supposed to do— help kids.

***

During this time, I ran into a guy from Boston, who told me he was a big fan of mine back east. His name was Dana White. He said he always stood up for me when some of the wise guys there would talk bad about me—about the time I pulled out on the Hagler fight. He seemed hungry, and I'm an expert when it comes to that. If there are a hundred people in a room and one is hungry, I will pick him out in a heartbeat.

I bought him something to eat and gave him some money for his pocket. I also took him to Propaganda Films and helped get him a job as a production assistant. He seemed so grateful, and I was happy I could be helpful to him. As I was leaving, Dana ran over to me with tears in his eyes and thanked me for the umpteenth time, and he hugged me. He told me he had an idea for a new style of fighting, put two guys in a cage and no rules, like street fighting. I thought, who the hell would want to see something like that? Whoops! He ended up training Mark Wahlberg, and a year later Dana's idea got Ultimate Fighting Championship skyrocketing through the roof.

* * *

Since then I have worked with a group of thirty ex-gang kids in Sylmar (a neighborhood in LA). All but one of them have turned their lives around. The one who didn't, stabbed me while he was high on meth. It was an inch from my heart, so I guess God had other plans for me.

Our group is now forming the Worldwide Organization to Aid Youth through Sports and Success Education. We will work with top boxing people around the world and organizations like Garden Pool, who teach people in fifteen countries around the globe how to create sustainable food sources by turning backyards and public spaces into chicken farms, fish ponds, and vertical hydroponic gardens. Our partner organization in Detroit, Detroit's Triple T Foundation, has been doing almost exactly the same things we plan for over four years, and is highly successful. We were recommended to them by Al Low, an old friend in the Boxing World who helped start a new Worldwide Organization to help reform the world of Boxing, starting with one country, the UK. In less than a year, they are now in thirty countries! In affiliation with the same people, my girlfriend, Barbara Gold, has been named Director of Media Affairs for the newly forming Women's International Boxing Commission. In fact, my title fight opponent, Jimmy Haynes, is working on this project with us. The business plan is unique. We will have a threefold strategy:

1. Promote boxing or other appropriate sports like soccer for energy level and fitness, plus what the UN calls "Positive Social Inclusion,"

2. Provide vocational training or setup businesses that will make each group self-sufficient by the end of the first year, and

3. Provide emotional quotient training—how to let go of some of the pain and negativity the kids have accumulated.

This positive energy is drawing serious investors, one being a man whose family is one of the major shareholders of one of the world's most prestigious hotel/casino investment corporations. He currently has an interest in doing a film about both my life story, and *François*, a movie about the time Frank Sinatra saved my life and a little boy helped me find my heart and soul again.

I hope to be able to write about the success of these and other endeavors, in the future.

PHOTOS

All photos from this book and more can also be found in the picture gallery at: **wbp.bz/survivalgallery**

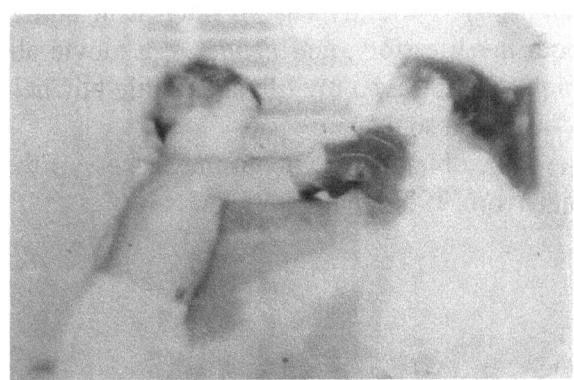

Vinnie Boxing with his Father at 2 Years Old

Vinnie's Hangout in Miami Beach – the Famous Restaurant

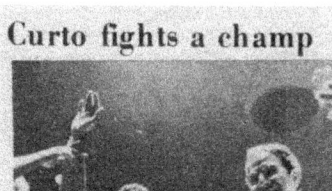

Curto Fights a Champ Article

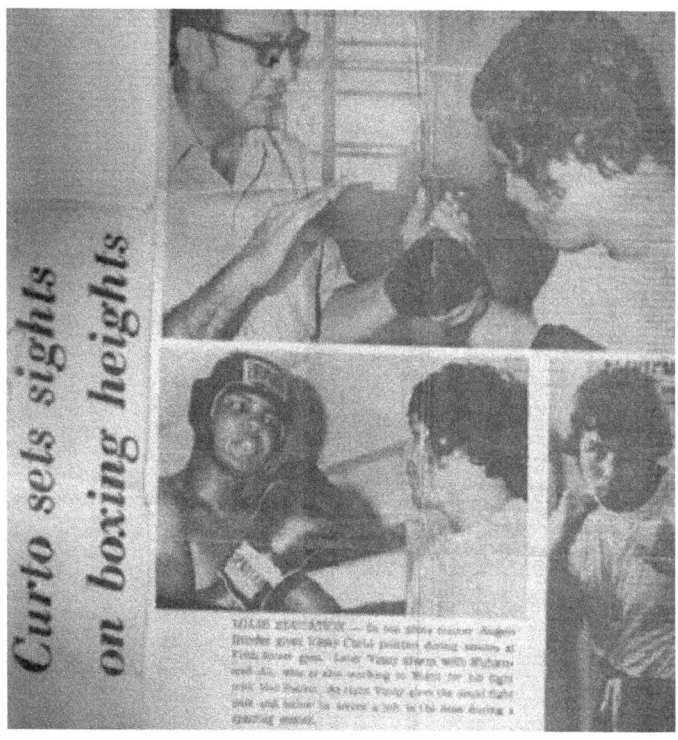

Vinnie Curto, Muhammad Ali and Angelo Dundee Article

Vinnie Curto, Angelo Dundee and Murry Gaby in Miami

Vinnie Curto and Bad Bennie Briscoe

Vinnie Curto showing his Name on Wall at Comedy Store

Sinatra Greeting Vinnie in Vegas along with Bob Botto

Vinnie Curto and Don Johnson

Vinnie Curto on Cover of World Boxing Magazine, "Champions of Tomorrow"

Vinnie Curto and Sherman Hemsley In AMEN

Vinnie Curto with Jim Moriarty and Title Belt

Vinnie Curto and Sylvester Stallone

Mark Wahlberg and Vinnie Curto

All photos from this book and more can also be found in the picture gallery at: **wbp.bz/survivalgallery**

INDEX

A

Aiello, Danny   *137*
Ali, Muhammad   *13, 51, 53, 173*
Anber, Russ   *100*
Anderson, Kelly   *107*
Anderson, Pamela   *146*
Antico, Pete   *137, 144*
Antuofermo, Vito   *65, 147*
Arum, Bob   *75*
Ayala, Roberto   *62*

B

Barajas, Zovek   *130*
Bernardi, Marciano   *103*
Bledsoe, Tyrone   *155*
Botto, Bob   *75, 83, 175*
Briscoe, Bennie   *63, 65, 68, 73, 110, 174*
Brown, Drew Bundini   *52*

C

Cami, Dick   *60*
Canalito, Lee   *124*
Carrey, Jim   *139*
Casado, Jeannie   *15, 27, 29*
Cassavetes, Nick   *137*
Classen, Willie   *81*
Clay, Andrew Dice   *139*
Clay, Marcel   *62*
Conforte, Joe   *126*
Conforte, Sally   *130*
Conteh, John   *61*
Cotroni, Frank   *103, 107, 109*

Curto, Jimmy   *10*
Curto, Loretta   *10*
Curto, Vinnie   *7, 10, 66, 81, 98, 110, 124, 156, 165, 173*
Cutler, Irving   *83*

D

Dangerfield, Rodney   *142*
Daniels, Terry   *60*
Davis, Sammy Jr.   *84*
De Niro, Robert   *143*
DePiano, Jimmy   *78, 81*
DiCaprio, Leonardo   *168*
Doaks, Torman   *161*
Dundee, Angelo   *13, 42, 44, 48, 63, 82, 130, 173*

E

Emmett, Sully   *44*
Esa, Lou   *62*

F

Faber, Claude   *103, 107*
Ferrara, Chickie   *64*
Fickling, Russell "Rusty"   *41*
Fillion, Jean-Yves   *99*
Foreman, George   *63*
Frazie, Mark   *129*

G

Gaby, Murray   *62*
Gacic, Casey   *58*
Garcia, Chucho   *64*
Giachetti, Richie   *124*
Gilmore, David   *126*
Giodano, John "Johnny Gio"   *70, 103, 110, 130, 132*
Gold, Greg   *143*
Goldstein, Mark   *140, 142*
Golin, Larry   *143*
Golin, Steve   *143*
Gravano, Sammy "The Bull"   *78, 81, 87, 97, 103*

H

Hagler, Marvin "Marvelous Marvin"   *34, 36, 63, 72, 74*
Haynes, Jimmy   *161, 170*
Hearns, Tommy   *131*
Hogan, David   *146*
Holmes, Larry   *53, 124*

J

Jackson, Cubby   *63*
Josephson, Barry   *141*

K

Kinison, Sam   *139, 142*
Kolkowitz, Joe   *136*

L

LaPaglia, Anthony   *137*
Larivee, Roger   *88, 99*
Licata, Tony   *64*
Longmire, Clinton   *130*
Lyle, Ron   *53*

M

Mann, Michael   *131*
Marion, Michel   *106, 109*
McCall, Jeff   *125*
McIntosh, Vernon   *57*
Melo, Eddie   *100, 107*
Migola, Charlie   *56, 132*
Migola, Roberto   *56*
Monzón, Carlos   *63, 73*
Moriarty, Jim   *153, 165, 177*

N

Negrete, Hector   *125*
Nicholson, Jack   *146*
Nicolella, John   *131*

P

Pacheco, Ferdie   *64*
Pacquiao, Manny   *24*

SURVIVAL | 181

Park, Chong-pal   *130*
Penn, Chris   *144*
Penn, Sean   *144*
Pep, Willie   *22*
Perez, Victor Taco   *55*
Pesce, Frank   *137*
Petronelli, Goody   *33*
Petronelli, Pat   *33*
Pinney, John   *65, 68*
Pondya, Rooshikumar "Rooshi"   *6, 101*
Primus, Barry   *143*
Pryor, Aaron   *155*

R

Ramsey, Bill   *99*
Rickles, Don   *84*
Rizzo, Jilly   *81*
Roach, Freddie   *24*
Rogan, Joe   *142*
Rolle, Baby Boy   *61*
Rondon, Vicente   *65*
Rossman, Mike   *78*
Rourke, Mickey   *51*
Royster, Dave Lee   *57*

S

Scott, James   *62*
Shavers, Earnie   *53*
Shields, Brooke   *137*
Silver, Joel   *141*
Simard, Réal   *109*
Sinatra, Frank   *81, 83, 171*
Small, Freddie   *14, 25, 70*
Stallone, Sylvester "Sly"   *124*
Sutherland, Murray   *131*
Swanson, Kathy "Trini"   *140*

T

Talhami, Chuck   *54, 64, 66, 151, 163*
Tyson, Mike   *124*

V

Valdez, Rodrigo   *63*, *73*
Valentine, Ernie   *157*

W

Wahlberg, Mark   *167*, *169*, *178*
Ware, Lamont   *161*
Waters, Dennis   *100*
Weinberger, Ed   *136*
White, Dana   *169*
Wilder, Deontay   *100*
Williams, Robin   *142*

AVAILABLE FROM ORI SPADO, DENNIS N. GRIFFIN, AND WILDBLUE PRESS!

THE ACCIDENTAL GANGSTER by ORI SPADO and DENNIS N. GRIFFIN

http://wbp.bz/taga

AVAILABLE FROM MONIQUE FAISON ROSS AND WILDBLUE PRESS!

PLAYING DEAD by MONIQUE FAISON ROSS

http://wbp.bz/playingdeada

AVAILABLE FROM KATHERINE ELLISON AND WILDBLUE PRESS!

MOTHERS & MURDERERS by KATHERINE ELLISON

http://wbp.bz/mothersmurderersa

See even more at:
http://wbp.bz/tc

More True Crime You'll Love From WildBlue Press

A MURDER IN MY HOMETOWN by Rebecca Morris
Nearly 50 years after the murder of seventeen year old Dick Kitchel, Rebecca Morris returned to her hometown to write about how the murder changed a town, a school, and the lives of his friends.

wbp.bz/hometowna

BETRAYAL IN BLUE by Burl Barer & Frank C. Girardot Jr.
Adapted from Ken Eurell's shocking personal memoir, plus hundreds of hours of exclusive interviews with the major players, including former international drug lord, Adam Diaz, and Dori Eurell, revealing the truth behind what you won't see in the hit documentary THE SEVEN FIVE.

wbp.bz/biba

SIDETRACKED by Richard Cahill
A murder investigation is complicated by the entrance of the Reverend Al Sharpton who insists that a racist killer is responsible. Amid a growing media circus, investigators must overcome the outside forces that repeatedly sidetrack their best efforts.

wbp.bz/sidetrackeda

BETTER OFF DEAD by Michael Fleeman
A frustrated, unhappy wife. Her much younger, attentive lover. A husband who degrades and ignores her. The stage is set for a love-triangle murder that shatters family illusions and lays bare a quiet family community's secret world of sex, sin and swinging.

wbp.bz/boda

www.ingramcontent.com/pod-product-compliance
Lightning Source LLC
Chambersburg PA
CBHW051548020426
42333CB00016B/2151